D1603294

CRESCENTS ON THE CROSS

ISLAMIC VISIONS OF CHRISTIANITY

CRESCENTS ON THE CROSS

ISLAMIC VISIONS OF CHRISTIANITY

Lloyd V. J. Ridgeon

OXFORD
UNIVERSITY PRESS

Great Clarendon Street, Oxford OX2 6DP

Oxford University Press is a department of the University of Oxford.
It furthers the University's objective of excellence in research, scholarship,
and education by publishing worldwide in

Oxford New York

Athens Auckland Bangkok Bogotá Buenos Aires Calcutta
Cape Town Chennai Dar es Salaam Delhi Florence Hong Kong Istanbul
Karachi Kuala Lumpur Madrid Melbourne Mexico City Mumbai
Nairobi Paris São Paulo Shanghai Singapore Taipei Tokyo Toronto Warsaw

with associated companies in Berlin Ibadan

Oxford is a registered trade mark of Oxford University Press
in the UK and in certain other countries

First published by Trinity St Mungo Press,
Faculty of Divinity, University of Glasgow,
Glasgow G12 8QQ, Scotland, in 1999.

This edition Oxford University Press, 2001
Reprinted by permission

ISBN 0 19 579548 2

Printed in Pakistan at
Shaheen Packages, Karachi.
Published by
Ameena Saiyid, Oxford University Press
5-Bangalore Town, Sharae Faisal
PO Box 13033, Karachi-75350, Pakistan.

Contents

Acknowledgements

I would like to express my gratitude to the Trustees of the Hastie Lectures for inviting me to deliver the Hastie lectures in May 1998. In particular, I would like to thank Alastair Hunter (Dean of the Faculty of Theology of Glasgow University in 1998) for suggesting ways in which I might undertake these lectures and for editing this work for publication. I am also grateful to staff and students at the University of Glasgow who commented on the lectures and provided new insights to the topics that enabled me to witness a horizon that I knew, but could not see, was ever expanding.

Dedication

This book is dedicated to Meevee, a friend whose enthusiasm knows no bounds

Introduction

Independent growth and development in any one region of the world is becoming increasingly difficult due the effects of globalisation, the influence of which has multiplied dramatically in the latter half of the twentieth century. Modernization and progress is becoming an international venture that requires comprehension of and respect for the diverse religions, cultures, and customs of the world. Yet levels of ignorance about the 'Other' remain depressingly high, a condition epitomized in an opinion poll taken in Britain which concluded that 80 per cent of the British public believed the greatest threat to the West came from Islam, following the fall of communism. (A. Ahmad 1992: 37). The situation from the Islamic perspective is similarly pessimistic, for Islamic scholars have stated that many Muslims who live outside the West tend to make generalizations about the beliefs of Western people. Either all Westerners are Christians or they are materialists, agnostic, and sceptics (Nasr: 1994, 136). Fortunately, some Muslims have been prepared to engage in a constructive dialogue with Western Christians, and atheists. For example, Mamadiou Dia, the former Prime Minister of Senegal has commented:

> Only a vigorous Muslim thought, endowed with sophisticated conceptual tools, can respond to the questions that the modern conscience poses. Contemporary Islam cannot content itself with the science of *hadith* [traditions of the Prophet] and *fiqh* [Islamic jurisprudence]: it must add to the traditional knowledge the knowledge of the great modern philosophies: religious philosophies, and secular philosophies.
>
> (Cited in Kurzman: 1998, 299)

Dia continues that Christian theology and atheist materialism do not necessarily destroy spirituality, but can contribute to a new 'Islamic humanism'.

Such encouragement directed at Muslims to investigate the essence of Christianity and secularism is indeed a positive development. The Islamic encounter with modern secularism is a recent phenomenon, and is considered by most Muslims a greater threat than Christianity to Islam. However, the relationship between Islam and Christianity dates back some 1,400 years, yet it is disappointing to find that even today certain Muslim attitudes to Christianity, and some Christian perspectives of Islam, reveal a distorted reflection of each others religion, a reflection that can be found in some medieval texts.

This book presents various Islamic perspectives of Christianity, and most of them adhere literally to the teachings of the Qur'an, which as a text, is open to a variety of interpretations. Some of these are developed and given palatable twists that provide optimistic grounds for those who are interested in nurturing co-operation, mutual understanding, and respect between the two religions in the modern age. Chapter one discusses two modern Islamic interpretations of Christianity, (those of Ahmad Khan and Mawdudi). The focus is primarily upon those issues that Muslims have investigated when analysing the 'weaknesses' of Christianity. These are the authenticity of the Gospels, the Trinity, and the crucifixion of Jesus. By studying the thought, life, and times of these two influential Islamic scholars it is possible to comprehend both the reason for the mistrust that some Muslims have for Christianity and Christians, and also for the need to forge some kind of rapprochement between the two religions.

The second chapter offers a means for Muslims to empathize with Christians. This can be achieved by meditating upon the mystical masterpieces of Jalal al-Din Rumi, who is regarded as the founder of the whirling dervishes. Rumi's poetry has more often than not been regarded as the embodiment of an 'inclusivist' Islam. There is a large degree of truth in this claim, and indeed, Rumi can be considered 'orthodox' in the respect that the 'inclusivism' of Islam is a doctrine that is grounded firmly in the Qur'an. The importance of the mystics of Islam is that they provide an ontological and epistemological framework for such a belief. So even if one concludes that Rumi was first and foremost a Muslim, this does not detract from the 'inclusivist' nature of Islam.

Chapter three presents a discussion on how Islam and Christianity perceive evil. To a large extent, the Christian understanding of evil is established upon the doctrine of Adam's original sin. The influence of Augustine's position on evil (that original sin is inherent in all men) has been far more dominant in the Christian tradition than that of Irenaeus who interpreted original sin in a far more positive manner. The Sufi understanding of evil, as portrayed by 'Aziz Nasafi, offers a similar and optimistic view of human nature, suggesting that Islam and Christianity need not drift in opposite orientations.

The final chapter describes the variety of interpretations that *jihad* (sometimes translated as 'Holy War') has undergone. Within this chapter, the Qur'anic, mystical, classical, and modern versions of *jihad* and their implications for the non-Muslim world are highlighted.

The aim of this book has been to focus on certain issues (in a general way) that are of significance in Muslim-Christian relations. Each chapter should be considered as an introduction to the issue in question, and those who are more interested in the specific nature of the subject will be able to investigate the topic in more depth by referring to the books listed in the bibliography.

1

The Views of Sayyid Ahmad Khan and Sayyid Abul A'la Mawdudi on Christianity

There are as many Islams as there are situations that sustain it (Al-Azmeh 1993: 1)

Two of the most famous modern Muslim reformers from the Indian sub-continent are Sayyid Ahmad Khan (1817–1898) and Sayyid Abul A'la Mawdudi (1906–1979). Ahmad Khan advocated the primacy of reason over a literal acceptance of scripture, and influenced by modern science and its use of reason, his works strode towards the 'universalisation' of individual rights at the expense of certain distinct Islamic beliefs. His use of reason resulted in him being labelled a *Mu'tazilite*[1] (Troll 1978: 37). Mawdudi also advocated the use of reason to modernise Islam, however, he was not as faithful as Ahmad Khan in following the path that the light of reason revealed. As a result, Mawdudi may be classified as a more literal interpreter of the Qur'an, indeed, some western scholars have labelled him a fundamentalist (M. Ahmad 1991)—though his Islamic opponents called him a *Kharajite*[2] and *Mu'tazilite* (Mawdudi 1952: 306).

The works of these two thinkers should be of interest to western readers because they provide examples of how some Muslims view Christianity (and by association, the west). Since the preferred exegetical method of each was different, one might expect that their attitude to Christianity would also differ. This chapter attempts to show to what extent, and why, if at all, Ahmad Khan's understanding of Christianity stands in contrast to that of Mawdudi. This analysis will be undertaken by focusing upon the historical circumstances of both Ahmad Khan and Mawdudi, and also by investigating their positions on three issues which have been at the centre of Muslim-Christian theological dialogue: the authenticity of the Gospels, the Trinity, and the crucifixion. In addition, their views regarding Muslims and the state will be described. All of the points mentioned above will be considered first in relation to Ahmad Khan and then to Mawdudi.

1 SAYYID AHMAD KHAN

India in the Nineteenth Century

Napoleon's invasion of Egypt in 1798 heralded the beginning of a new era in the Islamic world. More than ever before, Western European powers realized the economic and political importance of Islamic territories stretching from North Africa to India. During the course of the nineteenth century, the European powers were able to wrestle economic and territorial concessions from the rulers of the Ottoman Empire, Iran and India because of their superior industrial, technical, and military knowledge. It was in India, however, where western penetration was at its deepest, for in 1803, the great Islamic theologian in Delhi, Shah 'Abd al-'Aziz (d. 1824) implied in a *fatwa* that Islamic law did not prevail, but had been supplanted by Christian law. This being the case, India was now *dar al-harb* (literally, the land of war, which meant that it was no longer incumbent for Muslims to observe certain injunctions of Islamic law).[3]

In addition to interfering in matters of law, the British East India Company sought to maximize its economic activities, and also encouraged missionaries to undertake the 'moral improvement' of the Muslims and Hindus (A. Ahmad 1967: 25). Prior to the Indian Mutiny of 1857, many Muslims faced the challenge posed to them by Christian evangelical activity not through violence, but by engaging with Christians in theological argument. The Reverend John MacKay cites his own experience:

> Sometime ago a Muslim came to me, and in a very simple manner put the question, 'Does God know all things?' Of course I was bound to answer, 'Yes.' 'And is Jesus Christ God?' 'Yes,' I again replied. 'Then Jesus Christ must know all things?' As I did not know what the man was driving at, I again answered, with some hesitation, 'Yes.' Upon which, with an air of triumph, he quoted Mark 18.32: 'But of that day and that hour knoweth no man, no not the angels which are in heaven, neither the Son, but the Father.
> (Malik 1972: 193–4)

In fact dialogue between Christian missionaries and Muslims took place prior to the Mutiny, the most famous being the debates between the German K. G. Pfander (1803–65)[4] and Mawlana Rahmat Allah Kayranawi (b. 1818)[5] that occurred during the 1850s at Agra. The arguments offered by the Islamic side repeated the traditional 'weaknesses' of Christianity such as the incomprehensibility of the Trinity, the 'alteration' of the religious texts, and they also rejected the Christian emphasis on the importance of miracles (Powell 1976: 51–3). The significant point, however, is that the Muslims supported their arguments with reference to the works of Biblical scholars of the nineteenth century which admitted the existence of various readings and interpolations of the Bible.[6] Similar debates continued after the Mutiny, such as the two meetings held in 1875 and 1876 at Shahjahanpur, called the 'Festival of the Knowledge of God.' Yet, a real understanding of each others position was never really the objective, as B. Metcalf observes, 'Genuine intellectual exchange was thus irrelevant to the purpose of the debates. Each side could feel it had won because it simply judged its opponents by its own standards, and did not explore a different intellectual framework' (Metcalf 1982: 231). In participating in these debates, the Islamic community was largely reacting to the activities of Christian missionaries and those British administrators, such as W. Muir, who held that as the nineteenth century progressed, 'the dark incubus of idolatry, superstition and bigotry began gradually to receive the light and teaching of the Gospel' (Troll 1978a: 66).

In the wake of the Mutiny, Queen Victoria was established as head of India and all its inhabitants, and this divided the Muslims into several camps. The first of these was the position adopted by Sayyid Ahmad Khan who advocated loyalty to the British crown, since he believed that British rule was the destiny for India as decreed by God. In addition, Muslims and Indians could benefit from the justice offered by British rule: 'Of such benevolence as the English Government shows to the foreign nations under her, there is no example in the history of the world' (Khan 1993: 369). Moreover, he claimed 'British rule in India is the most wonderful phenomenon the world has seen' (A. Ahmad 1960–61: 65). Ahmad Khan aimed to raise the standards of Indian Muslims through education so that they could share in this wonderful phenomenon on an equal footing with the British. Thus, in 1877 he established the Mohammedan-Anglo College, which, based on English methods of education (Baljon 1949: 60), offered courses in arts, sciences, law, and languages. The opposition that Ahmad Khan faced in this endeavour was intense, for some Muslims believed that 'the study of English by a Musalman' came close to 'the embracing of Christianity' (Gandhi 1986: 33). Although not opposed to the study of English, the general political view of Jamal al-Din Asabadi, known as Afghani (1838–97) was diametrically opposed to that of Ahmad Khan. Afghani popularized the idea of Pan-Islam in his attempt to instil in Muslims sentiments of Islamic solidarity against European imperialism. Desiring to unite all Muslims, Afghani occasionally backed the efforts of the Ottoman Sultan, Abdulhamid, who claimed the Caliphate of all believers in Islamic territory. This claim was rejected by Ahmad Khan who advocated that India's Muslims should remain loyal to the British even if the latter's policy was detrimental to the Ottoman Empire (W. Smith 1946: 24). Somewhere between the positions adopted by Ahmad Khan and Afghani, were many religious scholars, and some established an Islamic seminary at Deoband near Delhi. The Deobandi '*ulama*' grudgingly accepted British rule[7] but aimed to bypass British laws and culture by educating and encouraging Muslims to preserve their own Islamic culture, and practice their own laws (Metcalf 1982: 146).

Ahmad Khan's Understanding of Christianity

In his attempt to forge a reconciliation between Islam and Christianity, Ahmad Khan realized that he needed to satisfy two audiences, namely the British and Muslims who supported Queen Victoria on the one hand, and the Muslims who rejected British imperialism on the other. The difficulty in achieving this goal resulted in Ahmad Khan saying one thing to one audience, and contradicting such views when addressing another audience. For example, on one occasion he wrote: 'My meaning is not that I am inclined towards their religion [i.e., Christianity]. Perhaps no one has written such severe books as I have against their religion, of which I am an enemy' (Khan 1993: 371). Yet in the majority of cases Ahmad Khan was at pains to show that Islam is not inherently hostile to Christianity:

> Among...unfounded reports is this, that the Muslims are by the tenets of their religion, *necessarily hostile to the professors of the Gospel of Christ*; whereas indeed the very reverse of this is the fact, for Islam admits, that there is no sect upon earth *but the Christians*, with whom its people may maintain amity and friendship.
> 'You shall find the most hostile people to the believers to be the Jews and the polytheists; and you shall find the closest in affection to the believers those who say: We are Christians. For among them are priests and monks, and they are not arrogant.' (5:82)
> (Khan 1993: 227)

In his attempt at placating the British and Christians, Ahmad Khan was very selective in citing the Qur'an. His *An Account of the Loyal Mohammedans of India* included only those Qur'anic verses which portray Christianity in a positive light. For example he quoted the Qur'anic verse cited above but failed to mention the negative descriptions which appear in 5:14–15 and 5:51.

If a rapprochement were to take place between Islam and Christianity, it would have to be established upon a firm basis, which was a thorough knowledge of the scriptures. Therefore, Ahmad Khan employed a Jew to teach him Hebrew, and he had access to the Gospels through Persian translations. His research resulted in three volumes entitled *Tabyin al-kalam*, a commentary on the Bible, and he is recognized as the first Muslim to have undertaken such a work (A. Ahmad 1960–61: 57). The first volume focused upon the Bible as a whole, the second on Genesis up to chapter eleven and the third commented on Matthew 1–5.

There are many issues upon which Islam and Christianity differ, but in this chapter the focus is upon three of the main points of disagreement. These are the authenticity or falsification (*tahrif*) of the holy scriptures, the Trinity, and the crucifixion of Jesus.

The first of the topics, the falsification of the scriptures has its origin in *sura* 2: 75 which refers to some Christians: '...a group of them did hear the Word of God, then after they understood it, they knowingly perverted (*yuharrifun*) it.' The deviation from the original Christian texts was an issue that was addressed by Christian scholars prior to Ahmad Khan's era. For example, T. H. Horne (1808–74) had argued that there existed different readings of the Bible, as well as interpolations. This suggested to Indian Muslims such as Kayranawi and his ally Wazir Khan that the Bible of the Christians was not the word of God. Wazir Khan indicated that one such interpolation was in the Authorized Version of the Bible, First Epistle of John 5:7, 'For there are three that bear record in heaven, the Father, the Word and the Holy Ghost: and these three are one.' Nineteenth and twentieth century scholars agree that this verse is not found in any manuscript prior to the fourth century and therefore it has been omitted from the Revised Edition of the Bible (Powell 1976: 57, n.31). However, nineteenth century Muslims of India believed this gave them sufficient ammunition to destroy the arguments of the Christian missionaries. As Muhammad Qasim Nanawtawi (1833–77), a leading Deobandi theologian explained, a drop of urine in a cup pollutes the whole (Metcalf 1982: 226–7).

Yet Ahmad Khan was more interested in reconciliation than refutation, and he indicated that there was much of value for Muslims in the Bible. *Tahrif*, according to him, aside from referring to a deliberate alteration of the scriptures, could also mean errors and mistakes appearing during the long transmission of texts. Therefore, it was necessary to undertake a historical and critical study of the original texts which would reflect the authentic revelation that was given to Jesus, and it is only this revelation which the Qur'an names the Gospel (*injil*). The Gospels of the New Testament, which were composed by the apostles (*harawis*), however, contained elements of the original *injil* when they quoted the words of Jesus. Ahmad Khan delved further in his attempt at finding some value in the Gospels of the New Testament, since he claimed that they were in fact a form of revelation (*wahy*)—which according to Islamic tradition is preserved for the prophets. Ahmad Khan made a distinction between the prophet's revelation and that of the apostle: the prophet's revelation is free from any mistake and may include commandments whereas the revelation of the apostle will not include commandments, and the truth of revelatory events may not be completely accurate. Yet, by attributing *wahy*, or a form of *wahy* to the apostles, Ahmad Khan was bending considerably away from the 'orthodox' Islamic understanding of the term. Such an idea, however, is not completely alien to Islam, for some of the Islamic mystics spoke of revelation (for prophets) and inspiration (for the so-called 'saints') as virtually interchangeable terms (Nasafi 1963: chapter 18). Yet, realizing that he was on dangerous ground may have persuaded Ahmad Khan to take a step back into orthodox territory by claiming that the revelation of the Qur'an was the words of God and as such, this revelation is a miracle. The revelation prior to the Qur'an, such as that bestowed upon Jesus (or the apostles) was of an inferior status because it did not represent God's words, but only the form of the content.

For the above reasons, Ahmad Khan believed that the Gospels of the New Testament confirm the Qur'anic message, and should not be dismissed as advised by some Indian Muslims such as

Kayranawi. The latter, knowledgeable of European Bible criticism of the nineteenth century, pointed out that the Gospels of the New Testament could not be relied upon since Luke and Mark were not apostles, the original Hebrew of Matthew was no longer extant, and the authorship of John was debatable (Troll 1978a: 83). Ahmad Khan was unable to accept these arguments and criticized in particular the works of F. C. Baur (1792–1860) who believed the Gospels of the New Testament were second century forgeries (Christie-Murray 1989: 195–6). Incensed to such a degree, Ahmad Khan remarked that Baur was a man whose 'heart is devoid of the Holy Ghost' (Baljon 1949: 122).

The second point of disagreement between Islam and Christianity concerns the Trinity. The Qur'an discusses a very strange form of Trinity to which the major, modern, Christian denominations do not adhere. The Qur'anic criticism of the Trinity in sura 5:116 seems to be directed at the idea of a holy family composed of God, Jesus and Mary. In addition to this, Islamic commentators concentrated on the Christian perception of the nature of Jesus. The Muslim position held fast to the Qur'anic doctrine found in sura 19 that Jesus was a man, albeit a rather special human, since he did not have a human father. Any claim to the divinity of Jesus is emphatically denied in the Qur'an.

Ahmad Khan's understanding of the nature of Jesus leaned heavily upon the arguments of the Islamic mystics, whose ideas were regarded with extreme caution by the more literally minded Muslim scholars. Inspired largely by the writings of Ibn 'Arabi (1160–1245), Ahmad Khan argued that the Qur'anic terms for Jesus, 'spirit of God' and 'messenger of God' mean the same as 'son of God' found in the Gospels. He states that God's act of creation is one of His eternal attributes, therefore the attribute of Jesus, as the Son, has also existed eternally. This discussion of Jesus in terms of one of God's eternal attributes has a long history in Muslim-Christian dialogue. For example, the Nestorian Patriarch Timothy I of Baghdad (d. 823) explained to the Abbasid caliph that the Word (i.e. Jesus) and the Spirit are inseparable from God, and resemble the attributes of reason and life which Islamic theologians used to characterize God (Thomas 2000). In addition to this, in his analysis of Jesus' nature, Ahmad Khan refers to Ibn 'Arabi's famous expression of *He/not-He*, which generally expresses the paradoxical reality of man's dual nature which in some respects is God-like, but in others is not God-like. Some Muslims scholars, remarked Ahmad Khan, said the same about Jesus, '*He/not-He*,' that is, 'he [Jesus] is [a human being] and he is not' (Troll 1978a: 97).

Ahmad Khan's understanding of the Trinity could not be accepted by Christians, for although the similarity of Jesus and God is recognized, so too is the authority of God over Jesus, which according to Ahmad Khan is explicitly revealed in Matthew 4:10 where Jesus rejects the temptations offered by Satan and proclaims: 'You shall worship the Lord your God and only Him shall you serve.' Moreover, Ahmad Khan states that if Jesus were God, Satan's efforts to tempt him would be pointless. The temptation only makes sense if Jesus is a man or prophet.

All of this led Ahmad Khan to the conclusion that the concept of the Trinity emerged as a result of the doctrinal conflicts of the early Christian community, which did not reflect the true teachings of the twelve apostles. By the sixth century, the message preached by Jesus had become so distorted that God had to send a new messenger, Muhammad, with the pure revelation (Troll 1978a: 99).

The crucifixion is the third point of disagreement between Muslims and Christians. Ahmad Khan accepted the Sunni tradition concerning the crucifixion that holds someone was crucified in Jesus' place, and Jesus himself was taken up to heaven before he died and will return to earth as the *Mahdi*.[8] (Interestingly, the Talmud contains passages which bear similarities to the Islamic version of the crucifixion).[9] Ahmad Khan suggests that Jesus may have been crucified, but he did not die and was taken down from the cross after three or four hours and concealed by his disciples who spread the rumour that he had ascended to heaven (Baljon 1949: 128). Moreover, Ahmad Khan adopts the classical Islamic position that Jesus' crucifixion was not necessary to redeem mankind because there is no concept of original sin in Islam. Adam was the first Islamic prophet, and since all prophets are considered to be immaculate, then his 'temptation' was a means by which humans would become responsible for their own deeds (Baljon 1949: 124).[10]

Conclusion to Ahmad Khan

One of the reasons that Ahmad Khan could not accept the Christian version of the crucifixion and resurrection was because of his attachment to human reason, or natural philosophy (cause and effect) in explaining the events that occur in this world. Impressed by the advances made by eighteenth and nineteenth century European scientists, Ahmad Khan stated: 'Gone is the age of faith during which everything, however strange, was accepted on authority. We now live in a new age—the age of scepticism—in which nothing can be accepted as true unless it satisfies human reason' (Zobairi 1983: 175). This belief in the law of nature caused Ahmad Khan to reject miracles, and also led him to understand angels, *jinn*, and Muhammad's Night Ascent (*mi'raj*) in an allegorical manner. He argued that any miracle of a prophet conforms to the laws of nature, which correspond with God's nature. However, he stated that there were thousands of events in nature, the natural laws of which cannot be explained because they transcend human understanding (Troll 1978b: 5). Ahmad Khan himself indicated that 'it is proved from the Qur'an that the Prophet did not bring forth any claim to miracles' (Zobairi 1983: 179).[11] Moreover, he claimed that if the sciences of the day are proved to be wrong, and new natural laws are shown to be true, then the Qur'an must be re-interpreted. Such a view means that scripture is (in the words of a contemporary scholar writing about Ahmad Khan) 'infinitely interpretable, and so, comes close to losing its sacredness and ceasing to be scripture' (Majeed 1998: 28). Because of this faith in natural law, and cause and effect, God is transformed from the hands-on, acting in time God of the Qur'an, to a remote, transcendent God, reminiscent of the God of the medieval Islamic philosophers such as Avicenna. Such a view has important practical implication for 'traditional' Muslims since it calls in to question the efficacy of prayer (Troll 1985: 36). Little surprise then that the more 'orthodox' Indian Muslims derided Ahmad Khan, labelling him a '*Nechari*' or Naturalist. In the words of Maryam Jameelah, one of Mawdudi's most vocal disciples, 'Although Sir Sayyid Ahmad Khan wanted to be considered an observant Muslim, his god was nineteenth century science and not that of the Qur'an' (Jameelah 1962: 83–4).

To a very large degree, Ahmad Khan's interpretation of Islam was due to the impact of western thought on India. Apart from the new scientific discoveries which forced Muslims to re-assess their beliefs, Christian missionaries also posed challenges on matters of ethics. Thus Ahmad Khan was obliged to address the existence of polygamy and slavery in Islam, and the answers he produced would have satisfied the Victorian British Èlite in India whom he was seeking to impress.[12]

The above has not provided exhaustive treatment of Ahmad Khan's understanding of Christianity. There are many other important points of Christian doctrine which he considered, such as the virgin birth which he denies, claiming that Jesus' disciples knew that Joseph was Jesus' father (Baljon 1949: 76), and he also criticized the impracticality of some Christian ethics, such as turning the other cheek (Baljon 1949: 122–3). However, the main points which have been outlined above explain why Ahmad Khan was, and still remains such a controversial Islamic thinker. Perhaps his most radical break with the Sunni tradition concerns his acceptance that Muslims can live in peace under British dominion. His aim in advocating this theory was to improve the position of Muslims in India after the Mutiny by demonstrating to the British authorities that Muslims could be loyal subjects. Referring to two books of Islamic law, he commented:

> It is stated in the *Hedaya* [*sic*] and *Alumgeeree* [*sic*] that when a Muslim enjoys protection and security under the rule of a nation not of his own faith, it is in the highest degree infamous if, from a professedly religious motive, he commits any outrage upon the person or property of those by whom he is governed.
>
> (Khan 1993: 232)

He provided the Qur'anic basis for this belief with reference to the Prophet Joseph who served the non-believer Potiphar, called by Ahmad Khan the 'King of Egypt'.[13] In a later work Ahmad Khan elaborated on the reasons why Muslims could live in peace within British India. Rather than being *Dar al-Islam* (the Islamic Realm of Peace) or *Dar al-Harb* (the non-Islamic Realm of War), India was *Dar al-Aman*–that is, 'the realm of security' in which Muslims could live according to the five pillars and also undertake Islamic preaching (Khan 1993: p. 321). In his own words:

> ...as long as Musalmans [*sic*] can preach the unity of God in perfect peace, no Musalman can, according to his religion, wage war against the rulers of that country, of whatever creed they be... Now we Mahomedans [*sic*] of India live in this country with every sort of religious liberty; we discharge the duties of our faith with perfect freedom; we read our Azans [call to prayer] as loud as we wish; we can preach our faith on the public roads and thoroughfares as freely as Christian missionaries preach theirs; we fearlessly write and publish our answers to the charges laid against Islam by the Christian clergy; and even publish works against the Christian faith; and last, though not least, we make converts of Christians to Islam without fear or prohibition.
>
> (Khan 1993: 301)

This being the case, *jihad* is unlawful since it can be carried out only against kafirs who 'obstruct the exercise of faith' (Khan 1993: 320). In fact, Ahmad Khan was not alone in adopting this position, for several religious clerics issued *fatwa* declaring *jihad* illegal when Muslims enjoy religious freedom (Friedmann 1989: 170–1). (Interestingly enough, a similar arguments was used in the 1940s within a short treatise entitled *Jihad* written by the founder of the Egyptian Muslim Brotherhood, Hasan al-Banna, whose influence upon later Islamic thinkers was considerable, especially upon Sayyid Qutb and Mawdudi).

It may not be too far from the truth to say that Ahmad Khan's understanding of Christianity and religion in general paved the way for future Indian Muslims to take the Muslim-Christian dialogue to its ultimate conclusion. For example, Amir Ali (d. 1928) believed that 'excepting for the conception of the sonship of Jesus, there is no fundamental difference between Christianity and Islam' (Ali 1891: 282). Professor Khuda Bakhsh viewed the new interpretation of Islam as indistinguishable from all true religions, and especially Christianity, which he frequently praised (W. Smith 1946: 32–3). Ahmad Husayn went further and boldly declared: 'True Islam is but true Christianity writ short' (W. Smith 1946: 37). Such views either glossed over distinctive Islamic laws or re-interpreted the 'traditional' manner in which they had been understood. Aside from his theological influence, Ahmad Khan's legacy can be witnessed in those who graduated from his Anglo-Muhammadan college, including Mawlana Muhammad 'Ali Jawhar (leader of the Khilafat movement), Khwaja Nazim (the Governor-General of Pakistan) and Liaquat Ali Khan (the Prime Minister of Pakistan 1948–51) (Symonds 1987: 30).

Those who rejected Ahmad Khan's response to the Christian missionaries included Mirza Ghulam Ahmad, the founder of the Ahmadi movement,[14] and more significantly, the educated Muslims typified by the Deobandi clerics who despised Ahmad Khan and everything he stood for. Indeed, he was slandered and persecuted, and the Mufti of Medina even issued a *fatwa* condemning him to death (Watt 1991: 102):[15] 'Sayyid was called a heretic, atheist, Christian, Naturist, materialist, unbeliever, the antichrist (*dajjal*), and in every town and village *fatwas* were issued against him by the Maulawis, which declared him to be a *kafir*' (Baljon 1949: 108).

2 SAYYID ABUL A'LA MAWDUDI[16]

India at the Beginning of the Twentieth Century

Events in the first couple of decades in the twentieth century ensured that the rapprochement that Ahmad Khan sought between India's Muslims and the British would be very difficult to achieve. British insensitivity to Islam was shown in 1912 over the

Cawnpore incident when the colonial authorities decided to demolish a mosque in order to widen a street (Baljon 1949: 43). More invidious to some Muslims was the outbreak of the First World War, which pitted the British (and thus India) against the Axis powers which included the Ottoman Empire. In other words, India's Muslims were expected to remain loyal to the British who were fighting Muslims of the Ottoman Empire. In addition, British behaviour during and subsequent to the war did little to foster good relations between the Christian and Islamic world. British duplicity was exposed in its encouragement to both Jews and Arabs to expect the right to establish a homeland-state in the holy land. This was followed by the dismemberment of the Ottoman Empire which was carved up somewhat artificially to create a series of British and French mandates, despite President Woodrow Wilson's insistence on self-determination. It is not surprising that in the Islamic world, scholars began to turn away from the liberal, democratic model of nationalism and political activity to the German version typified by the writings of J. G. Fichte (1762–1814) and E. M. Arndt, which is more inclined towards authoritarianism. The ultimate expression of the arrogance of some of the British, however, was played out in India at Amritsar in 1919 where the colonial forces massacred an estimated one thousand Indians (Moorhouse 1983: 226).

During the 1920s and 1930s the Indian nationalist movement developed and it included both Hindus and Muslims. Sayyid Abul A'la Mawdudi, however, did not consider himself a nationalist because this term was a western concept, having no basis in Islam. Writing in the late 1930s Mawdudi lamented that the religion (*din*) of Britain prevailed in India and 'Muslims' bowed their heads in obedience to Britain. It was necessary to return to the right *din*:

> ...if you submit to popular sovereignty, or to the Din of Britons or Germans, or to your nation and motherland, then again Allah's Din will have no place in it. But, if in reality, you are adherents of Allah's Din, there will be no room for any other Din.
>
> (Mawdudi 1982: 297)

Desiring to see the British leave India, and rather than witness the establishment of a Hindu dominated secular state, Mawdudi wanted to create an Islamic community in the whole of India, an aspiration which was somewhat unrealistic (S. Nasr 1994: 6). To give substance to this vision, he founded the Islamic Party (*Jama'at-i Islami*) which thrives to this day in Pakistan, India and Bangladesh.[17] Indeed, his version of Islam has been transported all across the globe, for Pakistani migrant workers have taken Mawdudi's ideas to the Gulf states of Arabia, and emigrants have established a branch of the *Jama'at-i Islami* in Britain (P. Lewis 1994: 100). In addition, Mawdudi's works were a major source of inspiration for other Islamic revivalists such as Sayyid Qutb (1906–66).[18]

The Islamic revivalism of Mawdudi rejected completely any of the western, secular ideas to transform and modernize the Islamic world. Thus communism, fascism, democracy and liberalism were all considered inadequate to resolve the spiritual, economic and political malaise of the peoples of Islamic territories. The panacea to all problems could be found in the pristine version of Islam, contained in the Qur'an, and in the example of Muhammad and the first four 'rightly guided' caliphs. This message is contained in Mawdudi's copious collection of writings, ranging from short newspaper articles to works of several volumes. One of his most famous works is 'Towards Understanding the Qur'an' (*Tafhim al-Qur'an*), an Urdu translation and commentary on the Qur'an, which he commenced in 1942 and finished in 1973.

The following presentation of Mawdudi's understanding of Christianity is based on the five volumes which have been translated into English (these translations cover chapters one to twenty-one—just over half of the Qur'an).[19] This commentary differs from those composed in the classical period of Islam in a number of ways. Firstly, the translation and literary style used by Mawdudi breaks with tradition. His intention in undertaking this *tafsir* was to bring the Qur'an to the 'average, educated person' who knew Urdu, and he admitted to adopting a 'relatively free interpretative rendering of the Qur'an' because literal translations 'lack literary force, fluency, eloquence, and stylistic charm' (Mawdudi 1988: I.1–2). Mawdudi did not consider it as a work for the Islamic scholars and religious clerics who could turn to numerous Arabic commentaries. Secondly, Mawdudi's *tafsir* is nowhere near as comprehensive as those composed by the likes of Zamakhshari (d. 1144) or Fakhr al-Din al-Razi (d. 1210) from the classical era, and 'Allamah Tabataba'i (d. 1982) whose microscopic examination of the Qur'an covered lexicography, syntax, etymology, and other specialist fields of study.[20] Nevertheless the significance of Mawdudi's *tafsir* lies in its brevity and limited scope because it is one of the most important channels through which the 'average' Muslim becomes acquainted with Islamic doctrine. It has been claimed that the *Tafhim al-Qur'an* is the most widely read commentary of the Qur'an in the modern era (Mawdudi 1988: I.xiii). Therefore, if one desires to understand how many contemporary Muslims perceive Jesus and Christianity, a thorough investigation of this *tafsir* will certainly provide a sound starting point.

Mawdudi's Understanding of Christianity

Mawdudi's discussion of the corruption of the Gospels differed from that of Ahmad Khan in the intensity of his criticism. For example, Mawdudi claimed: '[The Qur'an] is free from any trace of the ignorance, egocentricity, narrow-mindedness, iniquity, obscenity, and other corruption with which the Jews and Christians had overlaid their revealed Scriptures' (Mawdudi 1988: II.256–7). Despite such language, Mawdudi admits that scattered fragments of New Testament gospels are authentic, and such 'genuine' passages are those which begin with expressions 'And Jesus said' or 'And Jesus taught.' Moreover, if these fragments are analysed, it is clear that they do not contradict the overall message of the Qur'an, and any discrepancies can be resolved by unbiased reflection (Mawdudi I.234; II.178–9). There are three points contained in the *injil*:

first, man should serve God; second, this can be achieved by obeying the prophets; third, the first two points require an adherence to the laws that God sends via the prophets. According to Mawdudi, these three elements are found in the gospels of the New Testament: the first in Matthew 4:10, the second in Matthew 13:57, Luke 4:24 and Mark 6:4, and the third in Matthew 15:2–9 and Mark 7:6–13 (Mawdudi 1988: I.254–5). (His analysis, like that of Ahmad Khan, reveals a familiarity with the Old and New Testaments, which he quotes copiously, a practice that is rarely found in the treatises of classical and medieval Islamic scholars).

The second point of controversy between Muslims and Christians is the 'erroneous' belief in the Trinity, and this is the major concern related to Christianity in Mawdudi's Qur'anic commentary. His refutation of the Trinity is a mixture of arguments taken from the Qur'an, but also from western sources such as the *Encyclopaedia Britannica*, and in this, Mawdudi follows the tradition established in the nineteenth century by Kayranawi and Ahmad Khan. The main criticism levelled at Christians is one of excess in their belief in Jesus, which contradicts the Islamic doctrine of *tawhid* (the unity of God). The essence of *tawhid* is found in Jesus' advice in Matthew 4:10, 'You shall worship the Lord your God and Him only shall you serve' (Mawdudi 1988: I.255).

One reason explaining the appearance of that 'insoluble riddle' (Mawdudi 1988: I.117) which is the Trinity is the confusion over the miraculous conception of Jesus. Mawdudi states that both the Qur'an and the Authorized Version of the Bible confirm that Jesus was created of a spirit 'from' God.[21] This is in contrast to the 'orthodox' Christian understanding which speaks of the spirit 'of' God and thus deifies Jesus (Mawdudi 1988: II.116–7). Furthermore, Mawdudi adds that the conception of John the Baptist was also miraculous, and he states: 'Jesus' birth was no more miraculous than John's and there are no grounds for referring to John as God's son.' (Mawdudi 1988: V.157) Mawdudi drives this point further by stating that if Jesus is considered such a holy figure because he had no human father, then how should Adam be regarded since he had neither a father nor a mother (Mawdudi 1988: I. 260).

The confusion over the nature of Jesus was compounded by non-Christian sources. Mawdudi himself does not elaborate on this point but cites several lengthy passages from the fourteenth edition of the *Encyclopaedia Britannica* which argue that Jesus is regarded as a human in the Gospels, and that it was Paul and the influence of Jewish and Hellenistic teachings that transformed Jesus' original message (Mawdudi 1988: II.181–86).[22] Employing the same argument used by Ahmad Khan, Mawdudi claimed that Jesus' human nature meant that he could not save mankind. Indeed, there is no need for man to be redeemed in the Christian sense because the Qur'an states that God forgave Adam succumbing to Satan's temptation. So 'the stain of sin was washed away and therefore no stain remained–neither on Adam nor on his progeny–that might require that God's only begotten son be sent to the world to be crucified, as Christians claim, so as to expiate for mankind's sin' (Mawdudi 1988: I.66).

Stripped of his divine mantle, Jesus is regarded by Mawdudi as one in a chain of prophets sent by God to reconfirm the revelations that had been sent previously to mankind. Mawdudi points out several times that Jesus did not come to establish a new religion, rather, he abided by the Mosaic Law (Mawdudi 1988: I.254)[23] and his early followers worshipped in the temple of Jerusalem along with other Jews since they did not consider themselves separate from the Israelite community, nor deviating from the Mosaic law (Mawdudi 1988: II.146). Again, all of these points are made with reference to the books of the New Testament.

In some respects, this argument reflects the traditional Islamic understanding of prophetology. Beginning with Adam and terminating in Muhammad, the prophets deliver a message which is essentially the same: belief in one God, and the resurrection and judgement by God on the basis of man's acts. If any religious tradition does not include these articles of faith, then that particular tradition has been corrupted. This is the explanation Mawdudi offers for the absence in the Torah of the 'notion of Life after Death, of the Day of Judgement, and of Divine Reward and Punishment' (Mawdudi 1988: III.258).[24] Correcting the religious traditions is the reason for God sending the prophets, and the corruption that existed prior to Jesus included excessive piety, hair splitting arguments by the Jewish rabbis and the superstitions of the ignorant people (Mawdudi 1988: I.254).

Yet Mawdudi's treatment of prophetology blurs the differences found in various religions. Some Islamic scholars explained the differences with reference to the Islamic concept of *naskh*, or abrogation, referred to in the Qur'an.[25] God sends a prophet who abrogates the previous holy law that had been sent to man. Such a theory suggests a development through history until finally religion is perfected with the revelation given to Muhammad. Indeed, Ahmad Khan indicated that Jesus abrogated elements of the revelation given to Moses. He alludes to Matthew 19:8 where Jesus denies the permissibility of divorce even though it was allowed by Moses. Mawdudi, however, was 'disinclined' to accept this interpretation of abrogation (Mawdudi 1988: IV.364–5), even though there is an explicit reference to *naskh*, spoken by Jesus in *sura* 3:50 of the Qur'an:

> I will inform you concerning what you eat and what you hoard in your homes. In all this there is surely a sign for you, if you are believers!
> I have come to confirm what came before me of the Torah and make lawful to you some of the things that were forbidden to you. I have come to you with a sign from your Lord; so fear God and obey me.

Instead, Mawdudi understood *naskh* as highlighting a particular aspect of an issue at one time and emphasizing another aspect at another time. Two possible reasons explain this explanation of *naskh*. The first, is that it was the only possible logical result of his commitment to the unchanging revelation given to the prophets. Second, Mawdudi's brief and superficial examination shows that the issue of *naskh* during the twentieth century had ceased to be the controversial point of discussion that it had been during the nineteenth century when Christian missionaries such as Pfander held the idea that God could issue one command and then change it at a later date, in some way questioned God's wisdom and omnipotence (Troll 1978a: 91).

The weakness in Mawdudi's argument concerning *naskh* is all too apparent. In the Sermon of the Mount, Jesus says: 'You have heard that it was said to the men of old, "You shall not kill; and whosoever kills shall be liable to judgement". But I say to you that every one who is angry with his brother shall be liable to judgement,' and 'You have heard that it was said, "An eye for an eye and a tooth for a tooth". But I say to you, Do not resist one who is evil. But if any one strikes you on the right cheek, turn to him the other also.'[26] Clearly, Jesus is abrogating the Judaic law, and one presumes Mawdudi would accept these verses as authentic fragments of the Gospel because they record the speech of Jesus. Yet, Jesus' words are then abrogated by *sura* 2:190–91 of the Qur'an:

> And fight for the cause of God those who fight you, but do not be aggressive. Surely God does not like the aggressors.
> Kill them wherever you find them and drive them out from wherever they drove you out.

Such inconsistencies appear in Mawdudi's thought because 'of his apologetic posturing *vis-à-vis* Western thought' which caused him to stretch 'rationalism to its limits and, at times, found himself in rather untenable positions.' (S. Nasr 1996: 131).

The last point of disagreement between Muslims and Christians in this study concerns the crucifixion. Mawdudi denies Jesus' death on the cross and therefore the possibility of resurrection. However, his reason for doing this was not because it broke the laws of nature (for Mawdudi affirmed other miracles which the Qur'an attributes to Jesus), but since it would imply a more than human status for Jesus. Instead, Mawdudi accepts the Qur'anic account of the crucifixion of another individual whom the Jews had mistaken for Jesus. Instead of discussing the miracle which saved Jesus from crucifixion, Mawdudi proceeds to condemn the Jews for rejoicing as a result of their mistaken belief that they had killed Jesus. In his polemic against the Jews, Mawdudi accuses them of 'being behind almost every movement which arises for the purpose of misleading and corrupting human beings,' such movements including communism (since Marx was of Jewish origin) and the philosophy of Freud (Mawdudi 1988: II.111). Because of their disobedience,

> God has kept in store a painful punishment both in this world and in the Next for those Jews who have deviated from the course of true faith and sincere obedience to God, and are steeped in rejection of faith and rebellion against God. The severe punishment which has befallen the Jews in this world is unique and should serve as a lesson for all. Two thousand years have gone by and they have been scattered all over the world and have been treated everywhere as outcasts.
>
> (Mawdudi 1988: II.111–2)

Conclusion to Mawdudi

Mawdudi's consideration of Christianity does not offer anything new to the Islamic understanding of this topic. Yet his works are significant because their tone conveys a confident and self-assertive form of Islam which differs from that of Ahmad Khan. He points out that Islam can adopt the sciences that have developed in the west and Islamize them, thus making Islam strong again. This Islamization would prevent the ill effects of material prosperity that can result from modern science. In *Let Us Be Muslims*, Mawdudi states that such ill-effects are witnessed in Europe and America which have turned their backs on God's laws. This has caused high suicide rates, genocide, birth control, abortion, drug and alcohol abuse, jealousy, malice, enmity, the abuse of human rights, wife-swapping, and the production of nuclear weapons and poisonous gases (Mawdudi 1982: 81–4). It is generally held by social scientists that modernization has contributed to the European and American social malaise that Mawdudi highlights. However, Mawdudi's idealistic notion of the Islamization of modernity held that Islamic countries would not suffer the same problems experienced by those countries of Christian persuasion. The following comments of Nasr suggest why this may be so:

> The impetus for Mawdudi's exegetics was clearly sociopolitical: the Islamic revival was not intended to save individual souls, but to soothe anxieties born of social, economic, communal, and political crises before the Muslims of India. 'True' Islam was predicated on a different relation between mankind and God, one that was not private and inward-looking but externalized and engaged.
>
> (S. Nasr 1996: 63)

This is not the place to verify whether or not modernity can be Islamized without having to suffer the same problems experienced in the west. The point here is merely to show how Islam received an injection of confidence through Mawdudi's thought *vis-à-vis* the Christian-west. No where is this more apparent than in Mawdudi's discussion of *jihad.* At a time when opinion in India was moving towards non-violent opposition against British rule; criticism emerged against the Islamic concept of *jihad.* It was Mawdudi who responded to this challenge by publishing a book in 1930 entitled *Jihad in Islam.* The issue of *jihad* had arisen in India after 1924 when Ataturk had abolished the Caliphate which meant that many Sunni Muslims considered that they had lost their spiritual leader. Mahatma Gandhi and many Hindus had initially supported the Indian Muslims in their support of the Caliph because an alliance and good relations with Muslims would be of enormous assistance in the movement for Indian home rule. However, when the Caliphate was abolished some Muslims carried out acts of violence against Hindus, perhaps fearing the Hindu domination that might emerge in an independent India.

Yet Mawdudi's writings reveal that *jihad* should not be seen as 'a crazed faith...[when Muslims have] blood-shot eyes, shouting *Allah'u akbar* [God is great] decapitating an unbeliever wherever they see one, cutting off heads while invoking *La ilaha illa-llah* [there is no god but God]' (Cited in S. Nasr 1996: 74). However, he opposed an alliance with the Hindus because he viewed the secular, nationalistic ideals of the Hindu leaders as western inspired and contrary to Islamic law. He believed that if Muslims returned to the pristine version of Islam then Hindus would convert and the western threat would fade away (S. Nasr 1996: 54). His understanding of *jihad* then, is one of constant struggle to establish an Islamic order, a struggle which embraced all kinds of activity. The military element of *jihad*, however, was a weapon of last resort. Moreover, to criticisms that Islam was a religion spread by the sword, Mawdudi argued that after Muhammad's death, Muslims attacked the Persian and Byzantine empires to ensure the right to propagate Islam, just as the British claimed the right to spread Christianity in India. Here, there is a similarity with the argument of Ahmad Khan.

According to Mawdudi, *jihad* is the ultimate expression of Islam, it is the pinnacle of faith. This is because all other Islamic rituals, including prayer, fasting, paying the alms tax, and pilgrimage are considered to be a preparation for *jihad*, the aim of which is the establishment of God's laws in this world. If the *jihad* is successful, the result will be the assumption of power. Mawdudi points out the danger of power which is liable to corrupt, therefore *jihad* can only be carried out by those individuals who engage in the ritual prayer, fasting, paying the alms tax and pilgrimage in the perfect manner. Since these rituals are an expression of submission to God, the individual who submits completely will not be corrupted by power, and therefore can participate in *jihad* (Mawdudi 1982: 285–92). The conclusions he draws would hardly be palatable to non-Muslims because the ultimate goal of *jihad* is the establishment of Islam throughout the entire world:

> The objective of Islamic *jihad* is to put an end to the dominance of the un-Islamic systems of government and replace them with Islamic

> rule. Islam intends to bring about this revolution not in one country or in a few countries but the entire world. Although initially it is the duty of every member of the Islamic movement to work for revolution wherever he is, the final purpose is nothing but a world revolution.
>
> (Mawdudi, cited in Schleifer 1984: 98)

Yet Mawdudi stressed that this world Islamic revolution should come about peacefully, even though such a policy would involve suffering, imprisonment and perhaps martyrdom. He believed that *jihad* is justifiable if the preaching of Islam is restricted, if treaties are broken, and if Muslims are oppressed in non-Muslim territories (Schleifer 1984: 95). These conditions may be construed as a defensive *jihad.* The position of the People of the Book in this Islamic order can be deduced from his views regarding their status in his ideal Islamic state in Pakistan. People of the Book are offered protection, shelter and food, but they are not permitted any involvement in the running of the state, thus they are deprived of the vote. He legitimizes this idea with reference to the practice of Muhammad and the rightly-guided Caliphs who did not employ a single *dhimmi* in an important political, judicial or military position (Adams 1983: 122). The People of the Book are offered protection within the Islamic state if they pay the *jizya* tax (as opposed to the *zakah* tax which is levied on Muslims). This tax is then spent on the administration of the state which protects the rights of the People of the Book. However, in a polemical note, Mawdudi adds that one advantage of the *jizya* is that 'it reminds the *dhimmis* every year that because they do not embrace Islam, they are not only deprived of the honour of paying *Zakah*, but also have to pay a price—*jizya*—for clinging to their errors' (Mawdudi 1988: III.202).

GENERAL CONCLUSION

The investigation of Ahmad Khan's and Mawdudi's attitude towards Christianity has revealed that they both endorsed the Qur'anic positions on the Trinity, the crucifixion of Jesus and the *tahrif* of the scriptures. Despite this, it is clear that Ahmad Khan made a far greater attempt than Mawdudi to understand the Christian point of view, and this is demonstrated in his analysis of the nature of Jesus in terms of God's eternal attribute and his more sympathetic treatment of scripture. His ultimate rejection of certain Christian doctrines was not due to a committed faith in the literal word of the Qur'an, but rather to his belief in reason. This meant that Ahmad Khan was critical not only of some Christian beliefs, but also many traditional Islamic beliefs. Yet his criticism was not purely negative, for he encouraged constructive, rational dialogue between Islam and Christianity in the hope of the universal progress of society. Ahmad Khan was influenced by the historical circumstances of India in the nineteenth century, but this did not automatically determine his tolerant attitude towards Christianity. During his own life time there were Muslims such as Afghani and the Deobandi '*ulama*' who were less favourably disposed to Christianity and the West.

Mawdudi accepted the Qur'anic doctrine of the corruption of Christian scriptures, the rejection of the crucifixion and the criticism of the Trinity because, unlike Ahmad Khan, he had no desire to impress the British (and thus raise the social standing of Muslims). Indeed, there was no need to pay lip service to the British because by the 1920s and 1930s, concepts of self-determination and independence were already being discussed. Moreover, on all issues related to the Islamic worldview, Mawdudi was much more inclined to endorse a literal reading of the Qur'an than investigate alternative meanings through the imaginative and rational ways of Ahmad Khan.

At the beginning of this chapter, the difficulty involved in labelling Ahmad Khan and Mawdudi was considered briefly. One recent work, however, has stated forthrightly that Ahmad Khan should be regarded as an Islamic rationalist, while Mawdudi can be classified as an Islamic fundamentalist (McDonough 1984).

An analysis of Mawdudi's views concerning Christianity confirms this kind of classification, and his belligerent and insulting tone makes this apparent all too quickly. Even though Mawdudi claims that it is necessary to employ reason (not polemic) to reach conclusions, one has to agree with McDonough that there is an 'exaggerated claim to wisdom' (McDonough 1984: 110). Moreover, reason is not the primary tool of interpretation, for it has been shown in his discussion of abrogation (*naskh*), that Mawdudi falls into an untenable positions that contradict some of his other arguments. This being the case, one has to agree with H. A. R. Gibb's opinion that Mawdudi was 'writing to a predetermined conclusion' (Gibb 1947: 64).

This predetermined conclusion resulted in 'an ideology that is intended to be accepted or rejected as a whole package' (McDonough 1984: 109). Such a view emerged from Mawdudi's pessimistic view of humanity and history, since he viewed the decline of Islam as commencing after the time of Muhammad and the first four caliphs. It was therefore necessary to recapture the essence of this period and enforce that particular way of life. Given this, it is hardly surprising that Mawdudi did not view Christianity in a positive manner:

> The conclusion to which I have been led is that there is only one correct basis for morality and that basis is supplied by Islam. Here we get an answer to all the basic ethical questions and the answer is free from the defects noticeable in philosophic replies and untainted by other religious creeds which create neither firmness and integrity of character nor prepare men to shoulder the immense responsibilities of civilized life.
>
> (Mawdudi, cited in McDonough 1984: 61)

McDonough states that the world-view of Ahmad Khan was much more optimistic than that of Mawdudi. This was because of his belief in the primacy of reason:

> Then I asked myself how reason can with certainty remain free from error. I admitted that such certainty is not really obtainable. Only if reason is used constantly can the error of the reason of one person be corrected by the reason of a second person and the reasoning of one period by the reasoning of a second.
>
> (Khan, cited by Troll 1987a: 254–5)

This understanding of reason led Ahmad Khan to interpret the Qur'an in a liberal manner. It's specific laws were a response to certain historical circumstances, and as circumstances changed, so too should the interpretation of such laws. Using reason to judge specific laws of the Islamic tradition, Ahmad Khan concluded that Islam could be a religion worthy of the modern age. He rejected stoning, polygamy and slavery because although the abolition of such inhumane practices was not possible in Muhammad's time, circumstances in the nineteenth century had changed and demanded their prohibition. Although there can be little doubt that Ahmad Khan's views were influenced by the Christian morality of the Victorian era, his exercise of reason alone could have led him to the same conclusion.

In this respect, Ahmad Khan's thinking stands in contrast to that of Mawdudi. Indeed, by elevating reason to this lofty rank, Ahmad Khan believed that it was necessary to engage in dialogue with Christians, and rational discourse would help to ensure that people could live in a safe, equal, pluralist society. Such a society would be based on constitutional law, and although it would never be perfect, it would strive continually to reach this goal. At the other extreme was Mawdudi's belief in the perfection of society, which meant the imitation of the community of Muhammad, that is, Mawdudi's interpretation of that community. His perfected society would be deprived of various points of view, which inevitably would result in the emergence of an authoritarian leader.

The issue of how Muslims understand Christianity is not just a matter of theoretical debate. Mawdudi's polemic of sound and fury does indeed signify something to many Pakistani Muslims whose actions in recent years have revealed the depths of their intolerance towards Pakistani Christians. This is not to say there is a direct link between Mawdudi's writings and the attrocities committed by such Pakistani Muslims—such as the perpetuation of slavery, razing churches to the ground, rape and intimidation (*see* Scott-Clark & A. Levy, 1999: 29–36)—however, his works may contribute to the general political mood of modern Pakistan.

The practical implications came to the fore when in 1998, the first native bishop in Pakistan, Dr John Joseph, shot himself in the head as a response to a governmental law—promulgated in 1986 by President Ziaul Haq (himself an admirer of Mawdudi's thought)—that states, 'Whoever...directly or indirectly defiles the sacred name of the Holy Prophet Muhammad...shall be punished with death, or imprisonment for life'. 'Fundamentalists' have taken this law into their own hands, for a mob murdered a high court judge who overturned a lower court's blasphemy conviction.[27] What is needed in such situations is rational and calm investigation of issues involving Christians and Muslims, as advocated by Ahmad Khan, rather than Mawdudi's emotional and polemical attacks on Christianity.

NOTES

1. The school of *Mu'tazilites* emerged in the formative period of Islamic history. *Mu'tazilites* were theologians who emphasized the role of reason in understanding God, and they stood in contrast to what became the more orthodox position of accepting many seemingly contradictory statements in the Qur'an, (such as anthropomorphic verses, as opposed to those which stressed God's utter incomparability) without asking how.
2. *Kharajites* were Muslims who adopted a puritanical worldview, some of who believed it was legitimate to kill the Muslim who sinned. Recently, the term has been used by 'moderate' Muslims in Egypt to describe Islamic 'fundamentalists'.
3. A. Ahmad 1967: 19. There has been much debate as to whether or not this *fatwa* actually declared India to be *dar al-harb*, *see*, P. Hardy 1972.
4. *See*, Pfander 1986. This work was revised and enlarged by W. St Clair Tisdall in 1910. It is composed of three parts. The first argues that the Old and New Testaments are the word of God and that they have been neither corrupted nor abrogated. The second part sets forth the principle doctrines of the scriptures, aiming to show that their teachings are in conformity with the criteria of the True Revelation. The third part is 'a candid inquiry into the claim of Islam to be God's final revelation.' The polemical nature of this work is revealed in the contents of the third part which discusses whether the language and style of the Qur'an can be deemed to be miraculous, the miracles attributed to Muhammad, Muhammad's conduct, and the manner in which Islam spread.
5. For Kayranawi *see*, A. A. Powell (1993), chapter eight.

6. These scholars included D. F. Strauss who wrote *The Life of Jesus* and T. H. Horne, the author of *An Introduction to the Critical Study and Knowledge of the Holy Scriptures*. Strauss' work viewed the Gospels as portraying mythical rather than historical truth (Powell 1976: 53).
7. Deobandi 'loyalty' to the British was shown on such occasions as the death of Queen Victoria and coronation of the new king. (Metcalf 1982: 155).
8. The *Mahdi* literally means 'rightly guided one'. Although this term does not appear in the Qur'an, Muslims came to believe in the *Mahdi* as an eschatological figure who will re-appear as a renewer of faith for a short millennium before the Day of Judgement. The exact identity of the *Mahdi* is unknown although there are various interpretations. For example, Twelver Shi'-ite Muslims believe the Twelfth Imam is the *Mahdi*, while Sunnis hold that Jesus is the *Mahdi* who will return.
9. For example, Sanhedrin 43a discusses the trial and punishment of criminals and then states: 'If one of the disciples who argued for acquittal died, he is regarded as though alive and in his place.' Although this discussion is not specific to Jesus, 43a does indeed go on to discuss the 'hanging' of Jesus. *See*, Epstein 1987: 43a.
   In addition, Tosefta Sanhedrin states: 'Rabbi Meir used to say, What is the meaning of 'For a curse of God is he that is hung,' (Deut. 21: 23)? [It is like the case of] two brothers, twins, who resembled each other. One ruled over the whole world, the other took to robbery. After a time the one who took to robbery was caught, and they crucified him on a cross. And everyone who passed to and fro said, 'It seems the king is crucified.' Therefore it is said 'A curse of God is he that is hung.' *See*, F. E. Peters, 1990: 151.
10. Islam has a very different understanding of sin than those held in the Christian and Jewish traditions. With regard to the Jewish perspective of sin, Islam does not hold that the community suffers as a result of the sins committed by one's ancestors. Referring to a past nation of sinners, *sura* 2:140 of the Qur'an states: 'That is a nation which has passed away. It shall reap what it has earned, and you shall reap what you have earned. You shall not be questioned about what they were doing.' In his commentary on this verse al-Tabari says 'And you will not be asked about the actions which Abraham, Ishmael, Isaac, Jacob, and the twelve sons performed. For every soul which will come before God on the Day of Resurrection will be asked only about what it has acquired and advanced and not what others have advanced.' Cited by M. Schwarz 1972: 364–5
11. Ahmad Khan cites the Qur'an to argue his point: 'As God the Most High has said in the language of our Prophet, peace and blessings upon him, 'I am only a mortal like you. My Lord inspireth in me that your God is only One God.' [Q. 18, 110].' C. Troll 1978b: 5.

12. For Ahmad Khan on slavery and polygamy *see*, A. Ahmad 1967: 51–3.
13. Potiphar is not mentioned by name in the Qur'an, but appears in Genesis 39 as an officer of Pharaoh.
14. Mirza Ghulam Ahmad regarded Christianity as 'the most perfect manifestation of Satan,' and therefore, as Friedmann notes, the principal aim of his movement was to prove the superiority of Islam over Christianity (Friedmann 1989: 117–18).
15. Yet Ahmad Khan remained intransigent in the face of opposition: 'One should not be afraid of being declared a non-believer by a bigoted *mulla* (religious divine) because one refuses to believe literally such things as retribution in the grave, the ascension of the Prophet to Heaven, and the separate existence of Satan' (Zobairi 1983: 180).
16. Mawdudi was a distant relation of Ahmad Khan. Mawdudi's father had been sent to Ahmad Khan's Mohammedan-Anglo College at Aligarh although he was called back home when it was discovered he had been playing cricket and wearing western clothes).
17. For the Jama'at-i Islami *see*, M. S. Agwani 1996. For the Jama'at-i Islami in Bangladesh, see U. A. B. Razia Akter Banu 1996.
18. Mawdudi's influence upon Sayyid Qutb has been highlighted by G. Kepel 1985: 47–9.
19. The Urdu version was published in six volumes of about 700 pages, while the English translations that have appeared to the present contain five volumes of between 330 to 418 pages. For the English version see Mawdudi 1988–95.
20. On the *tafasi*r of these scholars, *see*, J. McAuliffe 1991: 37–89. In chapters three to eight, McAuliffe analyses various issues relating to the Islamic understanding of Christianity (*suras* 2:62, 3:55, 3:199, 5:66, and 5:82–83) by investigating the *tafasir* of nine writers. These commentaries are often detailed and lengthy, but if one examines the same *suras* in Mawdudi's *tafsir*, there is an exceedingly brief commentary on 2:62 and 3:55, and 5:66, and no commentary on 3:199 and 5:82–83.
21. The Qur'an 15:29 uses the preposition *min*, meaning 'from' (*wa nafakhatu fihi min ruhi*).
22. The articles cited by Mawdudi are 'Jesus Christ' by Rev. Charles Anderson Scott, 'Christianity' by Rev. George William Knox, 'Church History' (no author cited).
23. *See*, Matthew 5:17, 'Think not that I have come to abolish the law and the prophets; I have come not to abolish them but to fulfil them.'
24. Mawdudi's views reveal a lack of knowledge of the Old Testament. A notion of life after death appears in Job 26:5, 36:12 and in Daniel 12:2–3, 13.
25. Qur'an, 16:101, 'And if We replace a verse by another—and God knows best what He reveals—they say: 'You are only a forger.' Surely, most of them do not know.'

26. Matthew 5:21, 38. Ahmad Khan considered this teaching as impractical, but unlike Mawdudi he accepted the principle of *naskh*, and therefore could quite easily escape from this problem.
27. *See*, *The Independent*, 28.5.98, p. 17.

2

Christianity as Portrayed by Jalal Al-Din Rumi

Minstrel of the lovers, strum on the strings, strike fire into believer and infidel!
(Rumi 1957: no. 1156)

Jalal al-Din Rumi, also known as 'Mawlana' (Our Master) to Iranians, is considered to be one of, if not *the* greatest of Islamic and Persian poets. English translations of the works of this thirteenth century mystic have become remarkably popular in the contemporary western world to the extent that Rumi is 'reputedly the best-selling poet in America today' (Ernst 1997: 170). In its edition of November 25, 1997 the Christian Science Monitor reported that translations of Rumi's poetry exceed more than a quarter of a million copies annually.[1] The attraction of Rumi's works to western readers is surprising given the negative and misinformed understanding of Islam that is found in both the popular media and public opinion of Europe and the United States of America (Van der Mehden 1983; R. Fisk 1998). Indeed, after the collapse of communism, 80% of the British public believed the greatest threat to the West came from Islam (A. Ahmad 1992: 37). There are several possible reasons to explain the interest in Rumi's works in the West. First, Islam is the fastest growing religion in many parts of Europe, and it is only natural that believers will investigate the myriad literary manifestations of their faith, including Rumi's mystical masterpieces. Second, the West has become aware of Rumi's poetry through performances of Sufi dancing *(sama')* by members of the *Mawlawiyya* order which regards Rumi as its founder. The members of the *Mawlawiyya* order are the 'whirling dervishes' (whose *sama'* is accompanied with recitations and singing of Rumi's verse) and they tour major western cities on a regular basis.[2] Third, one of the general messages of Rumi's poetry is the need to transcend the boundaries that conceal the reality of things, and leave only the forms visible. Likewise, many people in the West are seeking a remedy for the alienation, social dislocation and spiritual void that they feel in the age of post-modernity. And it is within Rumi's works that such readers find verses that parallel their desire to transcend the restrictive barriers that their own cultures and environments have wrapped around them.

This third point, the need to cross over from the form of things to the underlying reality, is a common theme in Rumi's works. The following is a typical example:

> Lo, for I to myself am unknown, now in God's name what must I do?
> I adore not the Cross nor the Crescent, I am not a Magian nor a Jew.
> East nor West, land nor sea, is my home; I have kin not with angel nor gnome;
> I am wrought not of fire nor of foam, I am shaped not of dust nor of dew.
> I was born not in China afar, nor in Saqsin[3] and not in Bulghar;
> Not in India, where five rivers are,[4] nor 'Iraq nor Khurasan I grew.
> Not in this world nor that world I dwell, not in Paradise neither in Hell;
> Not from Eden and Ridwan[5] I fell, not from Adam my lineage I drew.
> In a place beyond uttermost place, in a tract without shadow or trace,
> Soul and body transcending I live in the Soul of my Loved One anew.
>
> (Nicholson, 1950: 177)

Verses of this nature that endorse an inclusive religion, however, provide a somewhat distorted picture of Rumi's whole message. One problem related to understanding the totality of Rumi's world view, which is particularly relevant to contemporary western readers, has been highlighted by Schimmel: 'Modern people tried to select from often very vague second-hand translations[6] only those verses that speak of love and ecstasy, of intoxication and whirling dance. The role of the Prophet of Islam plays in Mawlana's poetry is hardly mentioned in secondary literature' (Schimmel 1994b: x–xi)

Rumi was first and foremost a Muslim who viewed Islam as the perfect religion, indeed, *sura* 5:3 of the Qur'an states that Muhammad was sent to perfect religion, and *sura* 2:111–13 implies that Islam, as a universal religion, is superior to Christianity and Judaism. If one investigates Rumi's voluminous poetical works, it becomes clear that his understanding of Christianity reflects such Islamic tradition. Rumi's orthodoxy was described by Jami, the celebrated Persian theosopher and poet of the fifteenth century,[7] who portrayed Rumi's *Mathnawi* (a masterpiece composed of twenty-five thousand rhyming couplets) in the following manner: 'Whoever recites the *Mathnawi* in the morning and evening, for him Hellfire be forbidden! The spiritual *Mathnawi* of Mawlana is the Qur'an in Persian tongue.' (Schimmel 1980: 367) Moreover, according to Jami, this divinely inspired work almost raised Rumi to the rank of prophethood: 'Although he is not a prophet, he has a book!'

This chapter examines Rumi's attitude towards Christianity, and this should inform us of the nature of his inclusive religion. One of the problems in analysing Rumi's understanding of Christianity concerns the role of Jesus in his world view. Jesus is a multi-dimensional character in Rumi's works: sometimes he is the historical Islamic prophet; at other times he is a trans-historical symbol expressing the reality within each individual; occasionally he is the Christian Son of God. Therefore, in order to yield a comprehensive picture of Rumi's Christianity, not only is it necessary to analyse the explicit references he makes to Christian doctrine and practice, but a thorough investigation of the passages and verses that relate to Jesus is also required.

There are five sections in this chapter. The first presents a very brief discussion of the sources of Rumi's knowledge of the 'Christian Jesus'. Following this, the second section focuses upon how Rumi understands the 'Islamic Jesus'. From this basis, it is possible to proceed to the main argument of this chapter, namely, that by a careful analysis of his views of Jesus and Christianity, Rumi should be considered as holding an inclusive Islamic belief *with certain important reservations*. Thus, sections three, four and five provide examples: a comparison of Muhammad's prophethood with that of Jesus, criticisms of Christian doctrine and practice, and the nature of Rumi's pluralist vision.

1 RUMI'S KNOWLEDGE OF THE CHRISTIAN JESUS

The didactic stories that Rumi presents in his works indicate that not only was he fully aware of the Qur'anic portrayal of Jesus and Christianity, but that he had other sources which he utilised to portray Christian images. Such sources may have included the Gospels, but since Rumi lived during the thirteenth century, a period in which access to the Bible was difficult for Muslims (Lazarus Yafeh 1992: Chapter 4) his non-Qur'anic stories about Jesus may have been inspired by the *hadith*, the tales of the Prophets, the writings of previous Islamic scholars, or through verbal communication with Jewish and Christian communities. According to Schimmel, Rumi certainly conversed with the neighbouring priests and monks in Konya where he finally settled and established a Sufi *khanaqah* (Schimmel 1980: 180). There were Christian settlements in Konya from the earliest period of Christian history, for Saint Paul had attempted to convert the inhabitants of Konya (Iconium). Christianity continued to thrive in small pockets of Anatolia even after Islam had established itself there. Such Christian communities included Armenians and members of the Greek Church, some of who were descended from aristocratic Greek families and served the Seljuk rulers of Turkey. Rumi may even have come into contact with, or at least known about the more ascetic Christians who had settled in Cappadocia, which was within easy reach of Konya.[8]

Anatolia had also been on the Crusaders' route to the Holy Land, and no doubt the local Muslim population became more aware of certain Christian doctrines and practices during this period. Yet Rumi makes very few references to the Crusaders and their attempts to 'liberate' Jerusalem, because he aimed to discover the good in all things, including religion.[9]

Muslims might also have learnt something about Christianity through contact with merchants, the most famous European traveler being Marco Polo. Rumi's general positive attitude towards Christians was not mirrored by Marco Polo's opinion of Muslims:

> And marvel not that the Saracens hate the Christians; for the accursed law that Mahommet [*sic*] gave them commands them to do all the mischief in their power to all other descriptions of people, and especially to Christians; to strip such of their goods, and do them all manner of evil because they belong not to their law. See then what an evil law, and what naughty commandments they have!
> (Yule 1871: 69)

The references in Rumi's works to Jesus that bear resemblances to events described in the Gospels, but which do not appear in the Qur'an are not very numerous. There is a striking similarity between Rumi's story of Jesus not being allowed to remain in the jackal's den, causing him to proclaim, 'Lord, the jackal's whelp has a shelter, but the son of Mary has no shelter, no place where he may dwell,' (Rumi 1993: 54) and Matthew 8:20: 'Foxes have holes and birds of the air have nests but the Son of Man has nowhere to lay his head.' Another example can be found in Rumi's advice, 'When you get one blow on your cheek, go and seek another blow,' (Rumi 1925–40: VI, 930) which repeats Matthew 5:49. Mention must also be made of the association Rumi makes between Jesus and the donkey, a pairing which re-appears frequently in his works.[10] The donkey symbolizes man's body while Jesus—referred to as the spirit of God *(ruhallah)*, breath, word, and wind—represents man's higher faculties, such as reason or spirit. Jesus' entry into Jerusalem is evoked for Christians when Rumi comments that Jesus rode on a donkey out of humility: 'How else should the morning breeze ride on the donkey's back?' (Nicholson 1898: 17).

Other examples of Rumi's knowledge of Christian stories and incidents which are not mentioned explicitly in the Qur'an include the raising of Lazarus (Rumi 1925–40: V, 275–6), and Jesus' walking on water (Rumi 1925–40: I, 1185; II, 571–2). Christian images can be read into other passages of Rumi's poetry, yet it is necessary to be very careful not to miss the possible Islamic origin of such verses. For example, when Rumi exclaims, 'O seize the hem of his kindness!' (Schimmel 1994a: 103) or 'Lay hold of his skirt!' (Rumi 1925–40: I, 424; II, 344) the Christian reader might see associations of this with the story found in the Gospels when a women touches the edge of Jesus' cloak, seeking a cure for her illness.[11] However, most Sufis would be aware of the Islamic meaning in spiritual blessing *(baraka)* that can be derived from contact with sacred objects, while for Rumi it also refers to touching Joseph's shirt of the spirit, (Rumi 1925–40: VI, 4118) manifestly an Islamic image derived from the Qur'an (12:25–28). In addition, the phrase is also a Persian idiom that means 'to seek protection' (Arberry 1991b: 164).

2 RUMI AND THE ISLAMIC JESUS

Jesus is much more an Islamic Prophet in Rumi's oeuvre than the Christian saviour and Son of God. But Rumi is not content to list Jesus' miracles as portrayed in the Islamic tradition, rather he breathes new life into these stories, resurrecting them by unveiling a multitude of new meanings and insights which teach the Sufi path and lead the individual towards self-realization and intimacy with God. Rumi's portrayal of Jesus as an Islamic prophet is classified into four categories in this section.

Jesus as Spirit of God

The miracles of Jesus are frequently associated with the descriptions of Jesus as 'the spirit of God' *(ruhallah).* This name is derived from *sura* 21:99 which tells of God's spirit being blown into Mary who subsequently conceived Jesus. Likewise, Jesus is able to breathe life into objects, as *sura* 3:43–49 describes, he moulded a handful of clay into the form of a bird, and then animated the clay bird by blowing into it. Rumi interiorises this idea by describing how the Sufi shaykh can mimic the Messiah's act by transforming the spiritually dead Sufi aspirant through a single kiss on the lips (Rumi 1957–66: no. 1827; Arberry 1991b: 21).

Rumi's unceasing search for the realities behind forms, seeking to transform the dross into gold, leads him to use Jesus as Spirit of God with life-giving power as a symbol applicable to each and every individual. In fact, this connection is suggested in the *sura* 32:7–9 which states that the Prophet Adam was created from a mixture of earth and God's spirit therefore there is a degree of similarity between Adam and Jesus.[12] The name 'Adam' (*Adam* in Arabic) means 'man', thus Adam is considered the archetypal human being. So, if there is a degree of similarity between Adam and Jesus, there must also be a similarity between Jesus and each individual. The connection between Jesus and human beings lies of course in the spiritual dimension, and Rumi contrasts the divine realm (*lahut*) in which the spirit has its origin with the creaturely, corporeal realm (*nasut*):

> O my soul! You are like Jesus. O [what] good fortune you are for the Christian.
> You show the eternal realm of *lahut* through the realm of *nasut*.
> (Rumi 1957, no. 2617, line 27726)

Rumi compares man's spirit to Jesus and his body to Mary; the pains of the body (i.e. the pains that the body endures through spiritual effort such as fasting or devotional prayers) guide man towards the purpose of his creation, which is the meeting with

God. If man does not engage in spiritual and religious effort, then there is no chance for the Jesus of the spirit to develop:

> The body is like Mary. Every one of us has a Jesus within him, but until the pangs manifest in us, our Jesus is not born. If the pangs never come, then Jesus rejoins his origin by the same secret path by which he came, leaving us bereft and without portion of him.
> The soul within you is needy, the flesh without is well fed:
> The devil gorges to swelling, Jamshid[13] lacks even for bread.
> See now to the cure of your soul while Jesus is yet on earth;
> When Jesus returns to heaven all hope of your cure will have fled.
> (Rumi 1993: 33)

Aside from having reviving power, Jesus, or the spirit are also utilised as metaphors for rationality and gnosis, which seems somewhat contradictory given that the Sufis believed there was a certain tension between the finite capacity of reason and the infinite scope of mystical knowledge. Rumi states if Jesus (the spirit-reason) becomes the master of the donkey (the body), the latter becomes weak but is able to abide in the station of the men of reason. The individual whose donkey dominates over reason, however, finds that the former transforms into dragon. (Rumi 1925–40: II, 1858–60)

In contrast, the scope of the spirit is so great in acquiring knowledge that even eminent rational philosophers such, as Avicenna and Galen are left completely bewildered. Indeed, Avicenna would be like ‘a donkey on ice’ if he tried to understand the forms that appear ‘fatherless like Jesus’ in one’s breast (Rumi 1957–66: no. 35277). Furthermore, even though Galen possessed thousands of medical skills, they were pitiful compared to the healing powers of Jesus’ breath (Rumi 1925–40: I, 528).

Jesus’ Ascent

The second category concerns Rumi’s understanding of the crucifixion and ascent of Jesus. The Qur’an states that God caused another individual to take on the 'likeness' of Jesus, who was in fact taken up before his death to heaven.[14] Rumi follows the Islamic tradition of placing Jesus in the fourth heaven (Rumi 1925–40: I, 649).[15] (According to the eleventh century Isma'ili theosopher Nasir-i Khusraw, Jesus ascended to the fourth heaven because it contains the Sun, the heart of the universe, since it emanates light and heat which are the sources of life. Likewise, Jesus is a source of life because he revives the dead.)[16] Rumi reveals the spiritual reality that Jesus' 'ascent' holds for each person. Through religious effort, ascetic discipline and the cultivation of reason, the spirit is able to shake free from the shackles of the body (personified by the donkey), and like Jesus, soar upwards into the heavens even before bodily death:

> The situation of man is like this. They took the feathers of an angel, and tied them to the tail of a donkey, that haply the donkey in the ray and society of the angel might become an angel. For it is possible that he may become of the same complexion of the angel.
> Reason lent to Jesus pinions, and to heaven he flew and higher;
> Had his donkey had half a wing, he would not have hugged the mire.
>
> (Rumi 1993: 118)[17]

The following is another example of how Rumi gives everyday relevance to the images of Jesus and the fourth heaven, and the donkey and the stable. He compares a tyrannical king who orders the seizure of donkeys for forced labour with a just king:

> But the king [i.e., God] of our city does not take at random. He is discriminating. He is seeing and hearing.[18]
> Be a man! Don't be afraid of those who take donkeys: You are not a donkey. Don't be afraid, O Jesus of this age.
> Moreover the fourth heaven is filled with your light: God forbid that your station is in the stable.
> You are higher even than the sky and the stars, though for a good reason you are [temporarily] in the stable.
> The master of the stable is one thing and the donkey another: not everyone who has entered the stable is a donkey.
>
> (Rumi 1925–40: V, 2547–50)

Jesus' Miracles

Besides discussing Jesus as the Spirit of God, Rumi also describes Jesus' power to cure the deaf and blind, (Rumi 1925–40: III, 2585) and this ability to heal the sick is mentioned in the Qur'an in the same breath as Jesus restoring life to the dead (5:110). Rumi also speaks of the lame, the palsied, and those clothed in rags who gather outside Jesus' cell every morning in the hope of a miracle, and return home with their requests granted (Rumi 1925–40: III, 298–307). Another Qur'anic miracle is Jesus' ability to speak while still a baby, for which 'the most satisfactory parallel' is the Gospel story of Jesus lecturing in the temple when he was only twelve years of age.[19] Rumi adapts Jesus' Qur'anic words in *sura* 19:30–31, 'Lo! I am God's servant; God has given me the book and made me a prophet,' to demonstrate the real meaning of human perfection, personified in the following by the Sufi shaykh. Rumi plays on the doubling meaning of the Persian word *pir,* which as an adjective means old and as a noun signifies a venerable old man or a Sufi shaykh:

> Who is a 'shaykh'? He is a pir, that is to say, white haired. Do you understand the meaning of this hair, O hopeless one?
> If self-existence remains within man, then it is shown by the black hair [of existence].
> When his self-existence vanishes, man is pir whether he is black-haired or just greying.
> The existence of black hair is the attribute of man; it is not the hair of the head or beard.
> In the cradle Jesus says, 'Without having become a youth, I am a shaykh and pir!'
>
> (Rumi 1925–40: III, 1790–94)

The subject of colour introduces another of Jesus' miracles that Rumi presents in the *Mathnawi*. Jesus inserts a multi-coloured garment into a vat of dye and then draws out the same piece of clothing from the vat as pure and unicoloured. This episode appears in the apocryphal Gospel of Philip when Jesus entered the dyeworks of Levi and threw seventy-two colours into a vat. (R. McL. Wilson 1962: 39). Rumi's intention is to illustrate that the different forms of doctrine all have an underlying unity.[20]

The Master of Attributes

Finally in this section, Rumi's Jesus stories in *Fihi ma fihi* provide a possible juxtaposition of the Islamic concepts of divine mercy and divine wrath. Sufis of Rumi's era frequently expressed the mystical idea of the *coincidentia oppositorum*, where opposites become fused, or, all attributes are gathered together in one person who manifests each attribute at the appropriate time. This is the reality of the Perfect Man, in this case Jesus.

Taking divine mercy first, Rumi reports a discussion between Jesus who laughed much and John the Baptist who wept much. John questioned whether Jesus laughed because he had become secure against subtle deceits, and in return Jesus asked whether John had forgotten God's kindness and graces. At this point, one of the Friends of God wondered which of the two possessed the higher spiritual station. God replied to this inquiry in the words of a *hadith*: 'He who thinks better of Me—that is to say, 'I am where My servant thinks of Me'' (Graham 1977: 130). This is explained further in a discussion related to the Sufi understanding of the imagination (see below). God is the servant of each individual for he appears in the form that any particular person has of him. It is better therefore if God is imagined in the purest manner possible (Rumi 1993: 60–1).

Divine wrath is the subject of a question addressed to Jesus concerning the greatest and most difficult thing for a man in this world and the next. The answer given by Jesus is 'divine wrath' from which man can save himself by mastering his own wrath and rage (Rumi 1993: 60–1). The connection between Jesus and God's wrath also occurs in the *Mathnawi* when Jesus is found fleeing up a mountainside in an attempt to escape from a fool. Since Jesus has power over all things, the fool could not comprehend why he was running away, and asks: 'Whom do you fear?' (Rumi 1925–40: III, 2581). This episode has been likened to Jesus' temptation in the desert (King 1990: 84). While still attempting to escape from the fool, Jesus explains that folly is caused by divine wrath, which brings rejection in its wake. Rumi's intention in this story is to urge the spiritually minded to seek their own kind, and to stay away from fools who do not exercise their reason, who can obstruct the path to God.

The discussion concerning God's wrath and mercy is intriguing because one wonders whether or not Rumi intentionally meant to convey a teaching by juxtaposing these two attributes of God in narratives about Jesus. The answer would have to be negative if Arberry's opinion about *Fihi ma fihi* is correct, for he believed that it 'represent[s] the impromptu outpourings of a mind overwhelmed in mystical thought, the multifarious, and often arrestingly original and beautiful images welling up unceasingly out of the poet's overflowing unconscious' (Arberry 1993: 9). The stories themselves probably have no historical truth, and so Rumi could just as easily have used any other Islamic prophet, or combination of prophets to convey his teachings.

3 MUHAMMAD AND JESUS COMPARED

The Qur'an states the idea that all prophets are fundamentally the same, and that there is no distinction between them (2:136). So they can be considered perfect men who manifest the appropriate attribute at the correct time. Given this, Rumi poetically describes the perfect man of his age (such as Shams-i-Tabriz) as the 'Jesus of the Age' (Rumi 1953, no. 1156, line 12274), and he also employs the term 'Moses of the Age'.

However, Islamic tradition came to revere Muhammad over and above all other prophets since he was honoured with the revelation of the perfected religion. He is considered the most perfect 'perfect man', and this idealized Muhammad is very different from the Muhammad that emerges from a literal reading of the Qur'an. Indeed, it may be argued that after a literal reading of the Gospels, Jesus appears as a more remarkable prophet than Muhammad due to the detailed portrayal of the miraculous events in the former's life. Perhaps influenced by contacts with Christians, there developed certain traditions about Muhammad which are not mentioned specifically in the Qur'an.[21] Rumi, like other Muslims of his era, ascribed miracles to Muhammad, perhaps to counter those attributed to Jesus in the Gospels. Although the Qur'an states that Muhammad is merely a man who does not perform miracles (and that the only miracle of Islam is the Qur'an itself)[22] Rumi's works are littered with references to Muhammad's miracles. These include the splitting of the moon,[23] and God acting through Muhammad when he threw dust against his enemies.[24] Rumi also makes his comparison between Muhammad and Jesus explicit when he states that God honoured and brought Jesus before him, indicating to his creatures that whoever serves Jesus also serves God, however, God also did the same to Muhammad, 'manifesting by his hand all that he manifested by Jesus' hand and more' (Rumi 1993: 136).

Jesus' inferior rank as a prophet compared to Muhammad is referred to several times by Rumi. An example of which is Jesus' ascent to the fourth heaven which seems insignificant when compared to that of Muhammad who passed all the heavens, and spoke to and witnessed God, and then returned back to earth to continue his prophetic mission (Rumi 1957: no. 3685). Furthermore, Rumi compares Muhammad's 'Night Ascent' to walking through the air, whereas Jesus could only walk on water (an element considered grosser than air in the elemental hierarchy of the classical period). He describes the situation of a thirsty man who is carried along in the water of life:

> He is like Jesus, for the water carries him on its surface, since there is safety from drowning in the water of life.
> [But] Ahmad [Muhammad] says, 'Had [Jesus'] certainty been greater, the air would have been his carriage and he would have been secure,

> Like me, a passenger upon the air on the Night Ascent and sought divine communion.'
>
> (Rumi 1925–40: VI, 1186–88)

The reason that Jesus could not progress higher than the fourth heaven is explained by Rumi as a result of Jesus' possession of a needle. Although Jesus is portrayed as an ascetic who renounces all needs, and prefers seclusion in a cave or on a mountain, owning a needle reveals his lack of complete reliance on God for all earthly needs (Rumi 1957–66: no. 2550). Not all Sufis regarded Jesus' needle in such a negative manner. Hujwiri (d. 1063) relates that a certain shaykh was told by Jesus that the lights on his cloak were the lights of necessary grace. In other words, Jesus sewed upon his cloak each patch through necessity and God turned into a light every tribulation that he inflicted upon his heart (Hujwiri 1375: 56). Again, Muhammad's superior nature over that of Jesus is confirmed by Rumi who reports that 'Ali (Muhammad's son-in-law and cousin) said that his soul had been delivered from spiritual death due to the completion of Muhammad's prophetic mission. This was a feat that neither two hundred mothers, nor Jesus could achieve. Although Jesus could revive the dead such as Lazarus, ultimately they perished once again' (Rumi 1925–40: V, 274–6; IV, 1064–8).

In fact Muhammad is able to ascend to the highest rank because he is a kind of Islamic logos, created by God before time as the most perfect existent, containing all things within him. All prophets possess some degree of Muhammad's perfection, but cannot be said to encompass the completeness of the first and last prophet. (Rumi 1925–40: IV, 524–9)

> The Muhammadan Light was [divided] into a thousand branches...
> If Muhammad unveils even one branch
> A thousand monks and priests will rend [their] Christian belts.
>
> (Rumi 1957: no. 1137, line 12051–2)

The interpretation of the rending of the *'zunnar'* belt (which Christians were obliged to fasten around their waists to indicate their religion) may take several forms. On one level, the

Qur'anic revelation causes monks and priests to accept Islam, and thus cast aside the *'zunnar'* belt. On another level, it may be read as a criticism, not of Christianity itself, but of Christian monastic practice and celibacy.

Finally, mention should be made of Rumi's criticism of Jesus' practice of solitude or seclusion, which he implies is the origin of 'monkery' (to be discussed in the next section). A comparison is made between Jesus' solitude and God's command to Muhammad to be a guide for the community. Muhammad is like a second Noah, and should be the guide for all ships in their journey: he should not practice 'solitude like [Jesus], the Spirit of God', rather, he should put an end to 'seclusion and solitude'. (Rumi 1925–40: IV, 1458–62)

4 RUMI'S CRITICISMS OF CHRISTIANITY

Although Rumi's intention is not to criticize Jesus, following Islamic tradition, he does include verses which disparage Christianity. For example, Rumi refers to the malicious nature of some Christians in his narrative about the 'hypocrites' mentioned in *sura* 9:108–9, who built a mosque in Medina as a centre for spreading their anti-Islamic sentiments, and Rumi asks: 'When have Christians and Jews sought the welfare of the true religion?' (Rumi 1925–40: I, 2859). In addition, Rumi cites the Qur'anic story of the table in which the apostles ask Jesus for a table of food to be sent down from heaven, since this miracle would increase their faith.[25] God warns them that those who disbelieve after this miracle will be chastised. Some Christians fail to show respect when the table descends, for they hurriedly snatch away the viands, despite Jesus' pleas for them to restrain themselves, for the food is 'lasting' (Rumi 1925–40: I, 80–89; Qur'an, 5:65). Rumi sees God's chastisement of these people in *sura* 5:65: 'And He turned them into apes and swine'.

Aside from the malicious nature of Christians, Rumi's main criticisms of Christianity can be classified under three headings: a mistaken view of the nature of God, deficient practices, and falsification by Christians of the scriptures that God sends down.

The Christian Understanding of God

The monotheism that is so explicitly affirmed in the Qur'an is contrasted with the Christian concept of the Trinity that is described in *sura* 5:73. The Islamic mystical understanding of monotheism portrays existence as one (thus the boundaries delimiting man and God are erased). There is no concept of absorption with regard to man's mystical experience, since absorption occurs between two things. On achieving 'enlightenment', the Sufi has come to recognize that unity has existed all the time. This startling realization causes profound joy and peace in the Sufi, and results in mystics such as Hallaj, to reveal the secret of unity that contradicts the beliefs of those Muslims who witness an utter ontological chasm between man and God. In the following, Rumi associates multiplicity with Christianity, since multiplicity may be manifested in the form of the Trinity, or duality (an 'orthodox' Islamic criticism of Christianity, for Muslims held that Christians believed Jesus had both a divine and also a human spirit in one body):

> Become placeless in the Unity, make your place in the essence of annihilation;
> Every head which possesses duality put on a Christian neck.
>
> (Rumi 1957–66: no. 1876)

> The essence of the meaning of 'He' [God], my heart and soul has filled; He is—even though He said He is not—the third and second to me.
>
> (Rumi 1957–66: no. 207)

The proximity of God, or 'the Unity', is expressed in the following verse by Rumi, in which he appears to criticize Christians for not understanding that God is within the individual. There is no need for a priest to act as an intermediary between man and God. Although God exists within each individual, the divine cannot be encompassed, and this explains why God can initiate the attraction, or pulling (see below), which draws the individual towards the divine, or in other words, assists him or her to recognize Unity. Once this is realized, the water of life cascades from the once stone-like heart:

> The Christian confesses to the priest the sins of the year—fornication, malice, hypocrisy,
> So that the priest will forgive those sins, for he regards the priest's forgiveness as God's forgiveness.
> [But] that priest has no knowledge of sin and recompense ...
> When My pull is set in motion from [My] direction, [the Christian] does not see the priest intervening between [us].
> The Christian is craving forgiveness for his sins and transgressions from God's kindness behind the veil.
> When a spring overflows from a rock, the rock disappears in the spring.
> After that, no one calls it a 'stone', since such a [precious] substance gushes forth from the stone.
>
> (Rumi 1925–40: V, 3257–84)

Rumi's main criticism, however, remains with the Trinity. His remarks about the priest are designed to draw the reader's attention to his fundamental point, which is to realize Unity through love. Although Christian images are utilized in the above verses, Rumi also made the same point with reference to the Islamic jurist *(faqih),* who saw his task as analysing which human acts were legally permitted under Islamic law: 'Faqih! For God's sake, learn the science of love, for after death, where are 'lawful', 'unlawful' and 'obligatory acts'?' (Rumi 1957–66: no. 2705; Arberry 1991b: 63).

Related to this discussion of the nature of God, a lack of appreciation of the Christian conception of Jesus as Son of God is revealed in Rumi's comment, 'See the ignorance of the Christian appealing for protection to the Lord who was suspended [on a cross] ' (Rumi 1925–40: II, 1401). If Jesus cannot help himself, then how can he possibly help others? (Of course, Muslims have no need to believe in the crucifixion because the concept of original sin is a Christian one). Likewise, Rumi asks that after ascending to the fourth heaven, what can Jesus do for the Church? The answer for Rumi, is nothing, whereas the advent of Shams-i-Tabriz is the cause that sets the bed-stone of the mill in motion. (Rumi 1957, no. 114, line 1283–5).

Deficient Practices

'Monkery' was singled out in both the Qur'an 57:27 and *hadith* as a practice which was never prescribed by God. Rumi argues that monasticism is not sanctioned by God because religion is of a communal nature and faith is strengthened in a crowd. Despite their base nature, donkeys are exhilarated in a group and exert themselves. But when they stray alone, the road seems long and they become weary (Rumi 1925–40: VI, 514–15). In an explicit criticism of monasticism, Rumi spells out the communal duties of prayer, enjoining the good and forbidding evil, bearing the affliction that other people cause and conferring benefits on others (Rumi 1925–40: VI, 480–1). Rumi then warns that the person who wishes only for bread is a donkey, and companionship with such a person is the essence of monkery. (Rumi 1925–40: VI, 485). Indeed, Rumi contrasts the seclusion that he associates with monasticism with the warfare that is encouraged in some situations by Islam:

> ...Jihad occurs when a highwayman...is on the road,
> The valiant man enters the unsafe road to protect, help and battle.
> The root of manhood appears when the traveler meets his enemies on the road.
> Since the Messenger was the Prophet of the sword, his community is [composed of] heroes and champions.
> In our religion, war and terror are expedient; in the religion of Jesus [solitude in] cave and mountain is expedient...
> Generally a wolf seizes [its prey] when a lamb strays alone from the flock.
> ...He who has renounced the Sunna with the [Muslim] community, has he not drunk his own blood in the lair of wild beasts?
> The Sunna is the road of the community and is like a friend: without the road and without a companion you will fall into dire straits.
>
> (Rumi 1925–40: VI, 490–502)

Monasticism is associated in Islam with celibacy, which is considered in an unfavourable light. After all, writing does not come about unless it is through the union of ink and pen, and rush mats cannot exist until straws are woven together (Rumi 1925–40: VI, 521–23). Moreover, according to Rumi, monasticism does not resolve the problem of temptation because it is necessary to come face to face with temptation in order to master it:

> Don't tear out your feathers [O peacock], but detach your heart from them because the enemy is the necessary condition for this jihad.
> When there is no enemy, the jihad is inconceivable; if you have no lust, there can be no obedience [to the Divine Command].
> There can be no patience when you have no desire; when there is no adversary, what need for your strength?
> Don't be hasty! Don't castrate yourself, don't become a monk, for chastity depends upon the existence of lust.
> Without sensuality it is impossible to forbid sensuality: heroism cannot be displayed against the dead.
>
> (Rumi 1925–40: V, 574–78)

A similar message is provided in *Fihi ma fihi*, where the trials of the communal nature of Islam are compared with the problems encountered by Christian ascetics:

> The way of the Prophet now, may God bless him and give him peace, was this. It is necessary to endure pain, ridding oneself of jealousy and manly pride, pain over extravagance and clothing one's wife, and a hundred other pains beyond all bounds, that the Muhammadan world may come into being. The way of Jesus, upon whom be peace, was wrestling with solitude and not gratifying lust; the way of Muhammad, God bless him and give him peace, is to endure the oppression and agonies afflicted by men and women. If you cannot go by the Muhammadan way, at least go by the way of Jesus, that you may not remain altogether beyond the pale.
>
> (Rumi 1993: 99)

Other Christian practices that Rumi disdains include idol-worship: 'Infidels are content with the figures of the prophets which are painted and kept in churches.' (Rumi 1925–40: V, 3599). Rumi also has much to say about the consumption of wine which is forbidden by Islamic law. Perhaps because wine is not permitted by Islam, Persian mystical poets frequently utilized the image of a Christian wine-bearer who offers the intoxicating brew. Intoxication through the wine of love became a common theme in Sufi literature, and the metaphor was extended by describing the actions of the drunk who is unable to control his actions and ecstatic utterances *(shath),* such as the 'I am the Truth' uttered by Mansur al-Hallaj (executed in 922):

> O wine-bearer of the spirit! Fill that ancient cup, that brigand of the heart, that ambusher of religion!
> Fill it with the wine that springs from the heart and mixes with the spirit, the wine whose ferment intoxicates the God-seeing eye.
> That grape wine is for Jesus' community—but this Hallajiyan wine is for the community of the Qur'an.
> There are vats of that wine and vats of this. Until you break the first you will never taste of the second!
> That wine removes heartache from the heart for but an instant, it can never extinguish heartache, it can never uproot malice.
> (Rumi 1957–66: no. 933)[26]

The metaphor of the drunk and wine is continued in the following, in which Rumi identifies himself as the Christian wine-bearer, and his spiritual mentor, Shams al-Din al-Tabrizi (literally, the Sun of Religion of Tabriz), is the person who understands the secrets of wine:

> The actions of a drunk are caused by wine.
> What appears in water is nothing but [the reflection of the moon] above.
> At last, a cup from him, Tabriz, the Sun of Religion!
> Come, won't you tell just one secret to that Christian wine–bearer?
> (Rumi 1957, no. 2617, lines 27734–5)

The intoxicating effects of spiritual wine, as mentioned above, were often associated with Hallaj, and it is worthy to note that both Muslim and non-Muslim scholars have drawn two main connections between Hallaj and Christianity. First, Hallaj was accused of advocating incarnationism *(hulul)*, the infusion of two spirits within one body, a doctrine which Muslims held to be the Christian understanding of the reality of Jesus (that is, a divine spirit and a human spirit). Comprehending the message that Hallaj wished to convey is problematic, but as Ernst has indicated, Hallaj's poetic utterances such as 'My spirit mixes with your spirit, in nearness and distance, so that I am You, just as You are I', were criticized by his own friends because they seemed to 'imply a semi-Christian doctrine of incarnation *(hulul)*' (Ernst, 1985: 27). The second reason for the association between Jesus and Hallaj is that whereas the former is believed by Muslims to have escaped the cross, the latter met his end through crucifixion. Rumi contrasts the Christian belief in Jesus' crucifixion with the Sufi ideal of killing all non-Godly concerns associated with the lower self, or ego, which separates man from God:

> That idea the Christian carries abroad, the Muslim has not that idea, that he [God] is slaying the Messiah on the cross.
> Every true lover is like Mansur [al-Hallaj], they slay themselves.
> (Rumi, 1957–66: no. 728; Arberry 1991a: 78)

The reasons for Hallaj's execution remain somewhat obscure, although his controversial lifestyle, based on his interpretation and practice of Sufism, combined with with political intrigues of the Abbasid court certainly contributed to the decision to execute him. (Massignon 1994: 204–6). It seems that Hallaj himself was well aware of the consequences of his actions and the circumstances of his times, as he predicted: 'My death will be in the religion of the cross' (Ernst 1985: 69). Thus parallels have been drawn by western scholars such as Massignon and Mason of Hallaj's readiness 'to become a powerless victim, to suffer condemnation and death like Jesus, for the purification of his Community' (Mason 1995: 17).

Rumi also makes a parallel between Hallaj's ecstatic statement 'I am the Truth', and the story of Jesus who placed into a vat some clothes, which were then heard to exclaim: 'I am the vat' (Rumi 1925–40: II, 1347). In other words, both Hallaj and the clothes experienced the Islamic baptism mentioned in *sura* 2:138, which leaves individuals in the primordial nature.

Falsification (tahrif) of the Texts

The falsification of the texts was, and continues to be, one of the major topics of discussion between Muslims and Christians. *Sura* 2:75 accuses the People of the Book (Jews and Christians) of writing the Book with their own hands in order to sell it for a small price. The Qur'an does not offer specific examples of this, however, Islamic tradition identified the censorship of Muhammad's name from the Gospels as one instance of *tahrif*. In one of his narratives, Rumi claims that the name of Muhammad did indeed appear in the Gospels, in addition, the real Gospels foretold his battles, fasting and eating. This was recognized by a party of Christians who 'would bestow kisses on that noble name and stoop their faces towards that beauteous description' (Rumi 1925–40: I, 730). However, another group of Christians held the name of the Islamic prophet in contempt, and the corruption of their scrolls perverted the genuine laws and religion that God had sent down (Rumi 1925–40: I, 727–36). It has been suggested that this narrative alludes to the traditional Muslim belief that Muhammad is referred to in verses fourteen and fifteen of John's Gospel (Renard 1994: 145). Christians read *parakletos*, or advocate, whereas the Islamic belief is that the word revealed by God was *periklutos*, which means much praised, a name similar to the Arabic 'Muhammad' meaning 'one who is praised'.

Rumi's narrative of the appearance of Muhammad's name appearing in the Gospels is part of a lengthy explanation of how diversity appeared in the Christian community.[27] In this story,

Rumi portrays an evil Jewish king and his vizier who fail to see the underlying unity between the religions of Moses and Jesus, and in addition to attempting to discredit Christianity in numerous ways, they kill hundreds of thousands of Christians. In one episode, the vizier pretending to be a Christian, claims that he possesses the true message of Christianity, and he is accepted by the Christians as Jesus' deputy *(nayib-i 'Isa)*. Once in this position of power, this wolf in sheep's clothing hands to each leader of the twelve Christian communities a scroll that presents the 'pristine' version of the Gospels. The contents of these scrolls contradict each other, and in addition, the vizier privately appoints each of the twelve Christian leaders as his vicegerent *(khalifa)*. The vizier then commits suicide, throwing the Christian community into dissent and turmoil since each of the twelve communities regard their scrolls as genuine, and twelve individuals emerge claiming to be the true *khalifa* of the vizier. Muslims prior to Rumi were familiar with this story of the vizier and the Christians, the former being identified as Saint Paul. It has been argued that this identification was probably derived from Christian theologians favourable to Saint Peter.[28] One of the messages in this story is that Christianity in its true form is a genuine revelation from God. However, the twisting of the texts has caused the squabbles among the various denominations (reflecting *sura* 19:34–6) who fail to cross over from the form of religion to the inner meaning.

5 CHRISTIANITY AND SUFI PLURALISM

The essence of Rumi's message is the need to cross over from the form to the reality. Thus he speaks of 'a thousand Gabriels within man,' and 'the Messiahs within the donkey's belly,' and 'a thousand Ka'ba's concealed in a church' (Rumi: 1925–40: VI, 4584–87). Religions too have their form and reality including both Christianity and Islam. This is the basis of Rumi's pluralist world view that is established upon his mystical epistemology (derived in part from the writings of Avicenna). The knowledge that man obtains from this world through his five senses is stored in his memory, and can then be utilized by his imagination to give forms to abstract ideas. The imagination also plays a vital role for man in his understanding of knowledge that has its origin in the divine realm.[29] Such knowledge may be a self-disclosure of God (who is described in *sura* 24:35 as light), and the knowledge may be revealed by angels who are created by God from light. It is impossible for man to perceive God's light, and it is the imagination that enables him to make sense of God's self-disclosures and angels, since the imagination provides this light with a form. The imagination then is the store of forms that man has actualized during his life in this world, and the forms of the self-disclosures and angels will necessarily reflect his culture and upbringing. Rumi describes this process in *Fihi ma fihi* by comparing the human imagination to a vestibule of a house. Once the divine knowledge has entered the vestibule it can then become manifest in the world (Rumi 1993: 148–9).

Since everyone has a culture and a store of experiences that are unique to himself, Sufis could not limit God's self-disclosure through the imagination to a single form. Because the spirit transcends form, God is portrayed by Rumi as appearing in one form that is annihilated once it becomes an idol. In fact, some Sufis, including 'Aziz Nasafi (d. ca. 1300), described how the forms are annihilated each instant to be replaced by a new form, in the same way as a billowing ocean continually tosses up new waves (Ridgeon 1998a: 35). Such a view affirms God's infinite creative power, ultimate incomprehensibility and Sufi pluralism:

> Hold on to the skirt of His grace, for suddenly He will flee; but do not draw Him as an arrow, for He will flee from the bow.
> What images does He play at, what tricks contrive! If He is present in form, He will flee by way of the spirit!
> Seek Him in the sky, and He shines from the water like the [reflection of] the moon; jump in the water and He flees up to heaven.
> Call Him from the placeless and He points you to place, seek Him in place and He flees to the placeless.
>
> (Rumi 1957–66: no. 900; Arberry 1991a: 100)

To understand how Rumi considers pluralism, it is necessary to investigate the imagination further, and fortunately he offers many insights into this topic by employing themes which are relevant to Christianity. Several important features of the imagination appear in his explanation of the annunciation, an account of which appears in *sura* nineteen of the Qur'an. Islamic tradition holds that the spirit spoken of in the Qur'an refers to Gabriel who appeared in the likeness *(tamaththala)* of a man to Mary. In his discussion of the annunciation, Rumi has Gabriel explain that he is manifest to Mary through her imagination, and such forms which come from the unseen realm of God cannot be set aside, unlike the fantasies that derive from the transient human realm:

> Look well Mary, for I am a difficult form [to understand]. I am both the new moon and also the image (khayal) in the heart. When an image enters your heart and establishes [itself there], it remains with you wherever you flee Unless it is an insubstantial, false image that sinks like the false dawn. I am like the true dawn [created] from the Lord's light: no night prowls around my day.
>
> (Rumi 1925–40: III, 3773–6)

This appearance of Gabriel is merely the means by which God discloses himself. This occurs through the imagination, not in the realm of sense perception:

> All perceptions [ride] upon lame donkeys. He [God's self-disclosure] rides upon the wind, flying like an arrow.
> The eye of a child, like that of a donkey, falls upon the stable (*akhur*), while the eye of a man of reason takes account of the next world (*akhir*).
>
> (Rumi 1925–40: III, 3721; 3741)

At first, Mary did not understand the reality of this spiritual manifestation, and naked and fearful, she sought protection in God (Rumi 1925–40: III, 3704). Gabriel has to explain that although the external appearance of Mary's 'imaginalisation' is of a beautiful youth (thus the full moon) the inner reality is a manifestation of the divine attributes. Her fear and seeking protection in God is meaningless, as Gabriel elaborates:

> I am that seclusion that was [your] deliverance. You take refuge, yet I am that refuge.
> There is no greater calamity than not recognising [the Truth]: You are with the Friend but you don't know how to make love! You fancy that the Friend is a stranger. You have placed the name of sorrow upon a joy.
> This date palm, which is the kindness of our Friend, is our gibbet (*dar*), if we are robbers.
>
> (Rumi 1925–40: III, 3780–3)

The above verse is full of allusions to the Qur'an: 'seclusion' refers to Mary seeking isolation from her people before the advent of the spirit (19:17); 'refuge' is Mary's cry at the appearance of the spirit in 19:18; the 'date-palm' is mentioned in 19:23–25, when the pangs of childbirth drove Mary to a date-palm where she was able to eat and drink. It is interesting that Rumi also mentions a gibbet in the same sentence as the date palm, and it is interesting to speculate if Rumi is making an association with this tree and a crucifixion upon a tree? If God's self-disclosure through the imagination is not understood for what it is, then the person who misperceives the self-disclosure is like a robber who steals the image that does not belong to him. If this is the case, God's mercy turns to wrath, or the date-palm becomes a cross. A connection between 'imaginalization' and the crucifixion is offered by Rumi in another story when he describes a devious prince who desired to steal Jesus' crown. However the prince was crucified (literally, he became the crown of the gibbet *[taj-dar])* instead of Jesus (Rumi 1925–40: VI, 4367–68).[30]

Rumi was not the only Sufi of the medieval period to discuss God's self-disclosure appearing through the imagination. Indeed, on the basis of this kind of epistemological theory, Persian Sufis including Suhrawardi (d. 1191) and 'Aziz Nasafi held that experiences of non-Islamic people were legitimate manifestations of reality. However, there were other mystics who claimed that the mystical experiences of non-Muslims were deficient. For example, Najm al-Din Razi (d. 1256) held that Hindus, Christians, and Philosophers experienced the reality of the spirit 'whereas Muslims witness the lights and attribute of unity.' (Najm al-Din Razi 1982: 239, 289). His position was reflected in the writings of another Persian mystic, Ala al-Dawla Simnani (1261–1336), which record a hierarchy of seven spiritual centres within man, that is, seven levels of being which are differentiated by the 'spiritual witnessing' of colours (Corbin 1994: 121–44). These rankings reflect the hierarchy in the heavens, and Simnani places Jesus in the sixth heaven which is also the level attained by Sufis such as Hallaj. Simnani discusses the Christian mistake of believing that Jesus is God, and that of Hallaj which prevents further progression to the seventh station. For Hallaj, the experience of 'I am the Truth', that is, annihilation in God, caused him to think actual material absorption had taken place in the Godhead. The reverse is the case for Christians who believe that the Godhead was absorbed into the human. For Simnani, the reality of the sixth heaven is the appearance of the ego, or in other words, the breath, which God blew in to man, a reality which Hallaj and Christians misinterpret. The highest rank is the Muhammadan level, for here man realizes the nature of his essence which is derived from God's spirit. In other words, man is similar to, yet also distinct from God, a seemingly paradoxical situation that reflects the Islamic teaching of God's similarity and incomparability (or to use Christian terms, immanence and transcendence) with man.

Yet the position of Najm al-Din Razi and Simnani restricts God's absolute power; the famous light verse of the Qur'an (24:35) states, 'God guides to His light whomever He pleases.' The Sufis held that ultimately, regardless of the individual's actions, it is God that 'pulls' or attracts man to Him ('pulling' *(jadhba)* being one of the technical terms of the Islamic mystics). Numerous Sufis cited a *hadith* that supported this view: 'A single pulling of God equals all the works of *jinn* and men.'[31] Rumi also cites this *hadith* in a story of the famous lovers, Layla and Majnun. In Rumi's portrayal, Layla symbolizes God,

Majnun represents the spirit of the wayfarer searching for God, and a third party, namely a she-camel is introduced, signifying the body of this wayfarer. Both Majnun and the she-camel have their loves, for the former it is God, but for the she-camel it is her baby camel. Whereas Majnun desires to progress forward towards God, the she-camel wants to return to her infant. Since he can no longer control the camel, Majnun flings himself off the camel's back, but in doing so he breaks his leg. It is at this point that Majnun realizes that even after his spiritual effort he has to rely on God for any further progress, for 'such is the extraordinary voyage which transcends the utmost effort of the *Jinn* and mankind' (Rumi 1925–40: IV, 1555–60). Yet, in some passages Rumi implies that God's pull is more likely to occur if the divine commands and prohibitions are followed (Rumi 1925–40: VI, 1477–80). Christians also have divine commands and prohibitions revealed to them, and therefore it is possible that God will draw them to Himself. But one assumes that the Christian must follow the pristine commands and prohibitions, or else after the experience of pulling, he or she will become a Muslim. This is the position of 'Attar, a famous Persian poet in the generation preceding that of Rumi, who describes the conversion of Ma'ruf Karkhi (d. 815), a Christian who became a Sufi after receiving guidance from God's light (Meier 1960: 282). Once divine unity has been realized, and existence is understood in a mystical mode that is not comprehended through the senses, then all forms are transcended, and only pure Islam remains:

> I slept under the shadow of fortune; you [God] opened a way for me beside the five senses.
> On that road it is possible to go east and west without feather, without head or foot.
> On that road is no thorn of free-will; no Christian, no Jew.
> The soul, beyond the circumference of its blue sky, is escaped from blueness and blindness.
> Why do you weep? Go to the laughing ones! Why do you tarry? Go to the same place where you once were.
>
> (Rumi 1957: no. 2684; Arberry 1991b: 105–6)

CONCLUSION

This chapter has focused on Rumi's portrayal of Jesus and Christianity, which demonstrates that his inclusive interpretations of Islam must be reassessed. Certainly, there are many verses within Rumi's works that appear to endorse an inclusive interpretation, such as the following, which reveals how God may be manifested to believers of all traditions through the perfected individual:

> Sometimes, through your face you bestow love and impatience on reason:
> Sometimes, through your eyes, you play the Messiah to the sick.
> Sometimes, with your tresses you give the image of God's cord[32] to the believer,
> Sometimes through twisted curls you give a cross to the Christian.
> (Rumi 1957–66: no. 2498, lines 26410–1)

The above describes how reality appears in different forms, which is, perhaps, the major theme in Rumi's works: 'So long as the *form* of the Beloved's image is with us, for us the whole of life is a joyful parade' (Rumi 1957–66: no. 364; Arberry 1991a: 39).[33]

Yet, Rumi also considered that the Islamic form of religion was superior to others because its comprehensive nature extends into all spheres of life, including the communal nature of religion and worship. In this respect Rumi is an 'orthodox' Muslim, convinced that the form of religion was perfected with God's revelation that was sent to Muhammad. *Sura* 5:3 states: 'Today I have perfected your religion for you, and I have completed My blessing upon you, and I have approved Islam for your religion.'

For Rumi, everything in existence has a form and reality, and such an understanding can also be applied to Jesus. The form is the Jesus of the Qur'an, both a remarkable prophet who performed miracles and also the Perfect Man of the age who unites all attributes within a single person, reflecting the unity and multiplicity pervading the world. This Jesus is a saviour in as much as he calls people to the sacred law that God has revealed. To speak of Jesus in terms of salvation is meaningless for 'orthodox' Muslims because the Qur'an offers a version of Adam's fall and an interpretation of the nature of sin which are different from those in the Bible.[34] Accepting Jesus as a prophet will not redeem man. It is necessary to interiorize the teachings of the prophets, which can guide man to the reality within himself. For Sufis, it is the form of Jesus that Christians perceive in the Incarnation—an understanding in the sensory realm, not in the imagination.

The reality is the Jesus to whom Rumi refers as the 'Spirit of God', the 'Messiah within the donkey', in other words, it is man's spiritual dimension. This Jesus can provide salvation since he has the power to master the body and is the creative source that must be reflected in a mirror. It is necessary to witness the 'Jesus of your being' in the supersensory realm, the imagination. Each individual must become a mirror where the Truth can be witnessed as a theophany, just as light takes a form by shining through stained glass. This, according to Corbin, shows how 'the Godhead is in mankind as an Image is in a mirror. The *place* of this Presence is the consciousness of the individual believer, or more exactly, the theophanic Imagination invested in him. His time is lived psychic time. The Incarnation, on the other hand, is hypostatic union. It occurs in the flesh' (Corbin 1969: 275).

Generally Rumi's works reveal a deep reverence for Jesus as an Islamic prophet (as one would expect), and Christians do not 'remain altogether beyond the pale'. However the relationship between an idealized Jesus and Christians is summarised by Rumi thus:

> O Jesus the conjoiner [of *nasut* and *lahut*?]! The healing of great suffering,
> Don't guard the *zunnar* for the sake of two or three Christians.
>
> (Rumi 1957: no. 2220, line 23554)

NOTES

1. *See*, A. Marks, 'Persian Poet Top Seller In America.' 25th November 1997.
2. In December 1994, I attended a *sama'* of the whirling dervishes in the Cathedral Church of St John the Divine in New York.
3. *Saqsin*, according to Nicholson (1898: p. 282), was a city in the land of the Khazars whose territories extended from the Crimean to the Caspian Seas.
4. In Persian, *Panj-ab*, or *Punjab*, means the five rivers.
5. *Ridwan* is the doorkeeper of Paradise.
6. Schimmel (1980: 389) has noted that the verse cited above, *Lo, for I to myself am unknown*...does not appear in the critical edition of Rumi's works (ed. Furuzanfar 1957–66), but rather resembles the works of later Persian and Turkish poets.
7. 'Abd al-Rahman Jami (d. 1492), a great Sufi poet in his own right and commentator on the works of Ibn 'Arabi.
8. For Christians in Turkey during the medieval period *see*, C. Cahen 1968: 202–15. *See also*, A. Schimmel 1980: 180.
9. Reference to the Crusaders' capture of Jerusalem is made in the following:
   Though the Holy City has become filled with Frankish pigs, after all how has that brought the Holy Temple a bad name?
   (Rumi 1957–66: no. 1211, Arberry 1991a: 128).
10. The donkey is still regarded with disdain and ridicule in areas such as Iran and Turkey, perhaps because of the descriptions found of the donkey in the Qur'an. For example, 31:19 states, 'the most hideous of voices is the donkey's,' and 62:5 describes a people who do not understand God's revelations as donkeys that carry books. Rumi cites this verse (Rumi 1925–40: I, 3447).
11. Matthew 9:20, Mark 5:29, Luke 8:44.
12. Qur'an 3:58, 'Jesus in God's sight is like Adam; He created him from dust, then He said to him: 'Be', and there he was.'
13. Jamshid was a pre-Islamic Iranian king, famous for his love of pleasure. He was instrumental in introducing wine drinking into Iran. In this verse, the devil represents the body while Jamshid symbolizes the spirit.
14. *See*, Rumi 1925–40: VI, 4364–70, based on the Qur'an 4:154–9.
15. In some cases, the Islamic tradition holds that Jesus abides in the second heaven, and Ibn Ishaq (d. 773) cites a *hadith* to this effect (*see*, Ibn Ishaq 1955: 186).
16. *See*, S. H. Nasr 1996: 18. Medieval Islamic cosmology held that there were seven heavens (each one containing a planet) arranged around each other like the layers of an onion, with Earth at the centre. Beyond the

seven spheres were the fixed stars, and encompassing them all was the Sphere of Spheres. *See*, Fakhri 1983: 171–2. The idea of a living cosmos is found in the works of Plato and Plutarch, the latter considered the sun pumped out heat and light like blood. *See*, Sambursky 1987: 213.

17. According to Arberry (Rumi, 1993: 262) the verse is by Sana'i.
18. 'He is Seeing and Hearing' refers to *sura* 17:1.
19. For the Qur'an on Jesus speaking as a baby, see 19:30–31. *See also*, Parrinder 1995: 79. *See*, Luke, 2:49. It appears that the story of Jesus talking as a baby was quite common in Rumi's age. A variant was reported by Marco Polo, derived from the city of Saba (or Savah, some 50 miles southwest of Tehran). According to the story, three Magi, Jaspar, Melchior and Balthazar journeyed to worship a prophet that had been born in their time. Each of them had a gift; gold, befitting an earthly king; incense, suitable for God; and myrrh for a physician. On reaching their destination, one by one the Magi entered the dwelling where the prophet was. Each time, the child-prophet appeared in the form of an adult, seemingly of the same age as the Magi. (Yule 1871: 73–4).
20. Rumi 1925–40: I, 500–1. The root of transmission of this story may have been the Arabic Infancy Gospels (the dates of which have yet to be established, although it has been speculated that they might have been written in 400 CE). *See*, Parrinder 1995: 27–29. From there, it may have passed into the *Qisas al-anbiya* of Tha'labi (d. 1036) in which Jesus drew several garments out of the vat one by one and each was a different colour. The Sufi inspired poet Sana'i (d. 1131) offered an alternative in which Jesus dyed many coloured garments in his vat, and all the clothes become pure and white, *see* Renard 1994: 187–8, n.46.
21. As A. Jeffrey 1929: 393, comments: 'As pre-existence was ascribed to Christ, so it was to Muhammad. As Gabriel announced Jesus to the Virgin Mary, so he did to Amina, the mother of Muhammad. As the angel gave the name of Jesus before he was born, so in the case of Muhammad. As Jesus in infancy was presented in the Temple, so was Muhammad in the national sanctuary of Arabia. As Jesus in the beginning of his ministry had to pass through an ordeal of Satanic temptation, so did Muhammad. As Jesus chose twelve apostles, so Muhammad chose twelve companions. As Jesus ascended into heaven, so did Muhammad; and so on.'
22. Muhammad was considered *ummi* 7:157, which is generally understood in the Islamic tradition to mean unlettered.
23. Muslims believe *sura* 53:1 refers to this
24. Qur'an 8:17. Rumi discusses many other miracles performed by Muhammad, *see*, Renard 1984: Chapter 8.

25. As Parrinder comments, it is not clear whether this Qur'anic tale parallels the Gospels feeding of the five thousand or the Last Supper (Parrinder 1995: 87). Mentioned by Rumi 1957–66: 1739.
26. Rumi also tells a story in which Christian wine is considered in a spiritual light: *'In that* [Christian's] *wine there is a* [hidden] *spiritual substance, even as* [spiritual] *sovereignty is* [hidden] *in the dervish-cloak'* (1925–40: V, 3448).
27. For a discussion on this narrative see Dabashi 1994: 112–135.
28. *See*, Nicholson, 1925–40: 34–6
29. According to the Sufis, *sura* 18: 65 refers to this knowledge *('ilm ladunni).*
30. One wonders whether or not Rumi believed this likeness to Jesus occurred within the imagination of the Jews. The story of the prince again reflects the Qur'anic version of the crucifixion, since *sura* 4:157 states that the Jews believed they had crucified Jesus when in fact someone else who had a likeness to him was presented to them *(shubbiha la-hum)* and crucified in his place.
31. This *hadith* has been cited by many mystics including 'Ayn al-Qudat 1373: 47; Najm al-Din Razi 1982: 222; Nasafi 1973: 226.
32. Reference to *sura* 3:103, 'And hold fast to God's cord all together, and be not divided.'
33. Some of the best images within Rumi's poetry occur when he adopts an 'inclusive' approach:

    Every mote of my being is in love with your sun; take heed, for motes have long transactions with the sun.
    See how before the window the motes gracefully suspended beat; whoever has the sun for a qibla prays after this fashion.
    In the concert of the sun these mutes are like Sufis; no one knows to what recitation, to what rhythm, to what harmony.
    In every heart there is a different note and rhythm, all stamping feet outwardly, and the minstrels hidden like a secret.

    (Rumi 1957–66: no. 1195; Arberry 1991a: 127)
34. *Sura* 20:122 states that having succumbed to Satan's temptation, Adam repented and 'thereafter his Lord chose him, and turned again unto him, and He guided him.' In 2:38 God told Adam to leave the Garden but 'whosoever follows My guidance, no fear shall be on them, neither shall they sorrow.' Moreover, *sura* 2:140 comments that each person is responsible for his or her own actions and that the sins of one generation are not passed on to the next.

3

Islamic and Christian Traditions of Sin and Evil[1]

There is evil in everything good and something good in every evil.
(Shaykh Fadlallah,[2] cited in Kramer 1993: 551)

In the previous chapter, it was concluded that Sufis of the medieval period such as Jalal al-Din Rumi had interiorized the figure of Jesus to the extent that he became an ideal symbol of spiritual resurrection. However, as Rumi constantly points out, although there is a relationship between form and reality, one should not get confused into thinking that they are the same thing. Sufis understood the form of Jesus as a prophet whereas the reality of Jesus can appear for each individual within the soul. Christians hold that the reality of Jesus is Christ, the Son of God, a belief which is rejected by Muslims because of both the associations they see in this doctrine with divine multiplicity, and also because Jesus as Son of God is unnecessary for human salvation. In Islam there is no concept of original sin for the Qur'an offers a portrayal of Adam's temptation which contains several important differences from the Fall of the Christian tradition. These include Eve's complete innocence, and God's immediate compassion for Adam whose slip was not interpreted in Islamic tradition as original sin.[3] For Rumi, the reality of Jesus is latent within each individual, and through the exercise of reason it is possible for man to reach his own perfection. On the basis of this, God judges man according to his acts and faith.[4]

Although there are great differences in the Islamic and the Christian conceptions of both the Fall and also regarding the significance of Jesus which focuses primarily upon sin and evil, there are certain interpretations within both traditions which have elements in common, thus facilitating the dialogue between the two religions. These are the mystical understanding in Islam, and the version labelled 'Irenaean' by John Hick. The similarities between the two are centred upon an optimistic view of humanity and human destiny, something which we may need at the end of a century plagued with world wars, attempts at genocide, and turning blind eyes to problems of poverty and starvation.

Within the mystical tradition of Islam, there are numerous interpretations of sin and evil. Yet just one example is taken in this chapter to represent the Islamic perspective, namely the thought of 'Aziz Nasafi, a thirteenth century mystic. His views are interesting because they include many of the 'orthodox' Sufi ideas regarding sin and evil, but at the same time, he offers certain unique perspectives. Although Nasafi did not compose a single work devoted entirely to evil or sin, or suffering, his treatises contain many references to such topics and therefore it is possible to piece together his ideas on these themes. Moreover, due to the turbulent period in which he lived, Nasafi must certainly have pondered concepts related to evil.

His life spans the thirteenth century in Central Asia and Iran, when the Mongol hordes twice invaded the region. It is reported that during the capture of Nishabur in 1221, the Mongols constructed three mountains from the decapitated heads of their victims: one for men, one for women and another for the children. Moreover, Nasafi himself stated that he had to flee from Bukhara in 1273 as a result of an attack by the Il-Khan that accounted for the death of about 50,000 individuals. Therefore Nasafi was a first hand witness of evil, and his theories related to evil are worthy of our attention.

Likewise, the Christian tradition holds numerous interpretations of sin and evil, but this chapter focuses primarily upon the writings of Saint Irenaeus (c.130–c.202) which were popularized in the 1960s by John Hick in his *Evil and the God of Love*. In Hick's book two main theodicies of the Christian tradition were described, the Augustinian and the Irenaean. This chapter concentrates upon the latter because the possibility for a mutual understanding between the Sufi interpretation of sin and evil, and the Irenaean position is greater than that between the Sufis and the Augustinians. Irenaeus himself, as bishop of Lyons, was head of a Christian community that suffered imprisonment and martyrdom, and therefore like Nasafi, was no stranger to evil.

It also needs to be said that this study is far from comprehensive. The theme of sin and evil is such a vast topic related to many issues such as free-will and pre-determination, and punishment in Hell and reward in heaven. Although these topics are mentioned briefly in this chapter, the main theme is sin and evil and their connection with man and nature (that is, with the microcosm and the macrocosm).

1 THE FALL: EVIL IN THE MICROCOSM

The Christian Perspective

The theology of Irenaeus was largely a response to the challenges posed to 'orthodox' Christian thought from Marconians and various gnostic groups. The latter are of particular interest in the discussion of evil because they held that the material world, thus humanity, was largely evil. Moreover, the gulf between the unchanging transcendent God, or Being, and the corruptible, contingent evil of becoming was bridged by beings in the Divine Pleroma. In effect, the gnostics were at pains to remove evil from God, but in doing so, Irenaeus held that they had introduced a plurality of divine beings, whereas for him, the reality lay with one God.

Irenaeus desired to affirm the unity of God in such a way that would account for the existence of 'evil'. The problem he faced was to explain why, if God was good, all-knowing and all-powerful, did He create man knowing that he would sin, or disobey God. The solution was to interpret the 'Fall' of Adam in such a way that it was not really a 'Fall' at all, but rather a step in human development.

Adam and Eve were considered by Irenaeus to be children in the Garden of Eden, and the Fall was regarded as a childhood lapse due to weakness and immaturity; there is no concept of 'original sin' or the weakness of human nature. The basis for his idea was the distinction found in man as the 'image' of God and man as a 'likeness' of God. Genesis 1:26 states: 'Let us make humankind in our image, according to our likeness.' Inspiration was drawn from Paul in 1 Corinthians 45, 'Thus it is written, "The first man Adam, became a living being; the last Adam became a life-giving spirit."' Again in 1 Corinthians 49: 'Just as we have borne the image of the man of dust, we will also bear the image of the man of heaven.'

The first man (or first Adam) is portrayed in an undeveloped state, possessing reason and free will, and having the potential to perfect himself. Yet at this stage he is morally, spiritually and intellectually a child. The second man is actual, or perfected in the figure of Christ, who draws all men into a community of God-consciousness with himself (Hick 1996: 240). Since God is transcendent and infinite, it is impossible for creatures to witness Him, and Irenaeus refers to the story of Moses' encounter with God in Exodus, where God says: 'You cannot see My face, for man shall not see Me and live' (Irenaeus 1997: IV, 20.9). Since man cannot witness God with his bodily eyes, God in His generosity becomes visible for humanity, and this necessitated His revelation in human form through Jesus. Humanity then, is not a barrier between God and man, after all, Christ's humanity was the bridge between God and man. For this reason Irenaeus argued that it is possible for humans to be revealers of divinity, bearers of divine glory, and the means by which God is glorified (Minns 1994: 41).

The sin of Adam was a sin of disobedience, for he wanted to attain the likeness of God, or immortality, before he was mature enough to take on this likeness. If God had awarded this immortality to Adam as a child, Adam would not have reached his perfection, and he would have remained immortally disobedient. Therefore death was necessary for it would teach man that immortality was a gift from God, given when God willed and when man had developed. Jesus is the example of the perfection of humanity: he is the second Adam, the likeness of God attained, and through him death is defeated and immortality acquired. By Jesus' participation in all human stages, manifesting perfect obedience to God's will, the human race is redeemed.

	FIRST ADAM	SECOND ADAM
i.	Adam made from earth (no human father)	Jesus had no human father
ii.	Born of virgin earth[5]	Born of a virgin
iii.	Adam tempted by Satan	Jesus tempted by Satan
iv.	Adam disobeys at tree of knowledge on a Friday	Jesus dies on a tree on a Friday
v.	Head of the human race	Head of the Church

Figure 1

Irenaeus (Figure 1) points to several parallels between Adam and Jesus, but then indicates how Jesus made the right choice of obedience to God. He undoes what Adam did, and recapitulates (or brings together, or unites) all things in the way that the first Adam should have.

The Irenaean position thus shifts the guilt of sin or evil from Adam's shoulders somehow, for as a child he cannot really be blamed for his act. After all, young children desire to emulate their parents. Therefore the existence of evil in this world must be due to God, as part of his plan for man. His plan is, of course, the development of man from childhood to adulthood when man is able to appreciate the meaning of the likeness of God. Irenaeus claims that had Adam been created as a perfect individual, then his becoming would have ceased. However, this is impossible for creatures since they are always becoming. The only stable thing is God who is Being. Therefore God intended humans to be in a constant state of becoming, that is, in an infinite state of becoming like God (Minns 1994: p. 74). The emphasis, therefore, is away from a mystical and monist perspective since man is permanently wrapped in a fleshy body. This stands in contrast with the theosophy of Sufis such as Nasafi whose beliefs have been labelled 'monist' (Meier 1954).

In his conclusion to *Against Heresies*, Irenaeus reveals the extent of his optimism for mankind. As in Nasafi's theosophy, man is the telos of all existent things, superior even to the angels:

> For there is one Son who achieved the will of the Father, and one human race, in which are achieved the mysteries of God, the mysteries that 'angels desired to see' (1 Peter, 1:12) but they could not investigate the wisdom of God, through which his work was shaped and made concorporate with the Son. For God wanted his firstborn Word to descend into His creation to hold the Word and ascend to him, thus surpassing the angels and coming to be in the image and likeness of God.
>
> (Irenaeus 1997)

In his interpretation of the Irenaean position, Hick goes a step further and suggests that human development can continue after death. Fulfilling the 'wonderful potentialities [of humanity] ...normally requires more than the span of this earthly life,' the development must continue and be completed beyond this world (Hick, in Mesle 1991: 129).

The alternative to the Irenaean position that Hick discusses is that of the Augustinians who place the guilt of sin squarely upon Adam. God created man perfectly but somehow he sinned, a sin that was of his own doing and which cannot be attributed to God. There is no suggestion of human development, and therefore the whole view of man is much more pessimistic and dark than the Irenaean position. The latter, through the concept of human development, is able to defend itself from the criticism that an all-powerful, all-knowledgeable and merciful God would not have created an Adam destined to sin. The Augustinians, however, face great difficulties in answering the criticisms outlined above.

The Sufi Perspective

There is no better way to understand how the Sufis view the Fall and evil than referring to the explanations offered by 'Aziz Nasafi. His ideas are quite unique, and although I have not come across the same ideas in any other Islamic works, this does not mean that his ideas were unknown, indeed, copies of his treatises have been found in Turkey, Iran, Central Asia, China, India, Pakistan and Egypt.

Nasafi, like the Irenaeans, regards Adam's Fall in optimistic terms. It is not a Humpty-Dumpty Fall to disaster, but rather a Falling into love, a love for God. Just as Irenaeus portrays human development through the Fall, so too Nasafi presents a series of nine Falls leading to human perfection. For the Sufis, there are two possible routes to perfection. The first method is for man to look into himself, to see himself as he really is, for he is a mirror that reflects the divine attributes. This belief is contained in the famous *hadith* that states, 'God created Adam upon His own form' (Furuzanfar 1982: no. 346). The second method by which man can witness the perfection of existence is by contemplating the world, for this is also a mirror that reflects the divine attributes. The world is called the big man *(insan-i kabir)* and the macrocosm *('alam-i kabir)* while man is called the small man *(insan-i saghir)* and the microcosm *('alam-i saghir),* (Nasafi 1985: 45–6). According to Nasafi, the idea of these two mirrors reflecting the existence of God is contained in *sura* 41:53: 'We shall show them Our signs in the horizons and in themselves,' the horizons being the macrocosm and the selves being the microcosm (*ibid.*: 85–7). In this section, the relationship between the perfection of the microcosm and evil will be examined.

Adam's Fall is portrayed in a hierarchy of nine 'Falls' which correspond to the nine stages of divine creation. This commences from the first level of God's timeless knowledge of man, through the creation of the elements, the kingdoms of mineral, plant and animal, and then to man, who ascends towards his perfection by means of his intelligence and then is able to reach God through divine grace.

In each heaven there is a tree (Nasafi 1963: 302) and in the first heaven it is called the Tree of Possibility *(dirakht-i imkan)*. Here there is complete unity, for Adam and Eve are not opposed by Satan. However, when they approach the Tree of Possibility, they are compelled to leave this heaven because of the divine command 'Be!'[6] The reality of the first heaven is that it is the knowledge that God possesses of Adam and Eve (in other words, all possible things that exist only within God's mind, that is *in potentia*). When he commands Adam to 'Be!' the chain of being is set in motion, and the first building blocks of existence (which are the four simple elements and natures) appear in the world of phenomena. This is the second heaven, and the elements and natures have real existence as opposed to potential existence. The tree in the second heaven is the Tree of Mixture *(dirakht-i mizaj)*, and after being ordered out of this heaven Adam, Eve and Satan (who tempted them to approach the tree) reach the third heaven where the elements are mixed together to form compounds. Here the three kingdoms of mineral, plant and animal appear, and man is the most sublime kind of animal. However, at this level man is immature, for this is the stage of the ignorant and children where compulsion or restraint do not exist, nor is there anything lawful or unlawful. According to Islamic law, children are not responsible for their actions – they are not *mukallaf* – that is to say, they are unable to distinguish between right and wrong in an adequate manner, since their intelligence does not mature until they attain their adulthood. In the third heaven there is a Tree of Intelligence *(dirakht-i 'aql)* and when Adam came near the tree, God commanded that Adam, Eve, Satan, the Devil, the peacock and the snake should leave this heaven and live in the fourth heaven.[7]

It is here at the Tree of Intelligence that God addresses Adam and tells him not to remain stationary in the path or become distracted by pleasant or unpleasant things, but to start walking, or ascend towards the pinnacle of the hierarchy. After all, the Qur'an states that God told the angels that He knew something about man that they did not, which Nasafi interprets as the potential to reach the reality of God. From this point in the fourth heaven, Adam possesses intelligence, the distinguishing characteristic of mankind, therefore his aim is to become a perfect man. In the fourth heaven exists the Tree of Mankind *(dirakht-i khalq)* and it is through free-will and the experiences associated with choice that man acquires knowledge and enters the fifth heaven which has a tree named the Tree of Knowledge *(dirakht-i 'ilm)*. The fifth heaven is as far as Adam can journey on his own for this is the limit of intelligence. Asceticism and laborious religious effort pay no dividend and any further progress in the hierarchy is a result of God bestowing his mercy or his light *(nur-i allah)* upon man.

At this stage, we enter the realm of mysticism proper, for it is a station where God is experienced directly without the restrictions and definitions that intelligence stamps upon things. The tree of the sixth heaven is called the Tree of God's Light, and the wayfarer may be bestowed with this light in order for him to journey into the seventh heaven which has a tree named the Tree of Encounter with God *(dirakht-i liqa')*. Finally, in the eighth heaven is the Tree of Power *(dirakht-i qudrat)* which leads to the ninth heaven. The distinguishing feature of this level is that man has the ability to create, or perform 'charismatic powers' such as walking on water or flying through the air (*see* Figure 2).

HEAVEN	REALITY OF THE HEAVEN	TREE IN HEAVEN
First Heaven	God's knowledge.	The of Possibility, leads to the Second Heaven.
Second Heaven	Creation of the elements and natures (earth, water, air, and fire).	Tree of Mixture, leads to the Third Heaven.
Third Heaven	Creation of the three kingdoms (mineral, plant and animal).	Tree of Intelligence, leads to the Fourth Heaven.
Fourth Heaven	Creation of humans.	Three of Mankind, leads to the Fifth Heaven.
Fifth Heaven	Humans reach the level of intelligence where they have the ability to Confirm the prophets.	leads to the Sixth Heaven.
Sixth Heaven	Man now has the ability to commence his spiritual journey towards God.	Three of God's Light, leads to the Seventh Heaven.
Seventh Heaven	Human intelligence can only go so far, from where God may bestow His light upon the individual in which case the journey continues.	Tree of Encounter with God, leads to the Eighth Heaven.
Eighth Heaven	Man reaches God and witnesses Him.	Tree of Power, leads to the Ninth Heaven.
Ninth Heaven	Man is able to perform charismatic powers, such as walking on water, or flying, etc.	

Figure 2

Perfection of the microcosm is reached at the ninth heaven, yet this is only a relative perfection, since perfection rests with the infinite existence of God. Since man is finite, the relatively perfect individual comprehends something of this infinity. In most cases for perfect individuals, the first twenty years of life are the period for perfecting the body and the subsequent twenty years are for perfecting the spirit.[8] Thus, man may become perfect when he is forty years old, the age at which, according to Islamic tradition, Muhammad received revelation from God (Schimmel 1994: 82).

The absence of evil in these nine 'Falls' is conspicuous. Nasafi stands the whole idea of Adam's Fall on its head, for he sees each Fall as an ascent *(mi'raj)* to a higher level. This return to God reflects the Islamic belief in the ascent (also known as the night journey) of Muhammad, who was taken by night from his bed in Arabia to Jerusalem.[9] From there he passed through the heavens and reached God's Throne where he spoke to and listened to God without an intermediary. Nasafi's nine levels correspond to the Islamic cosmological view of the seven heavens that are mentioned in the Qur'an.[10] Two levels are added, and these form the summit of the hierarchy, that is, God's footstool and God's throne (associated with the fixed stars—or the stars of the zodiac—and the sphere of spheres, which encompasses all of the other concentric spheres).[11] The first three 'Falls' or 'ascents' have nothing to do with Adam as man, since he is not involved in the bestowal of existence upon the possible things, or the advance from simple elements to compounds. It is only with intelligence (which necessitates the existence of free will) that Adam can propel himself forward as far as the sixth heaven where he ultimately has to rely on God if any further progress is to occur.

The idea of evil emerging as a result of the misuse of free will is apparent in Nasafi's discussion of Adam and Satan as they exist within the microcosm. The microcosm is the summary of the macrocosm thus it contains within it everything that exists in the macrocosm (including Adam and Satan). Adam is represented in the microcosm as man's intelligence, so if man does not act on the basis of his intelligence, then he becomes Satanic, since Satan is proud and disobeys God's command. If man acts on the basis of intelligence, then he becomes angelic, since angels obey God's commands and thus man is able to receive knowledge from the invisible world (Nasafi 1963: 10,

17). Nasafi discusses how God's deputy, that is intelligence (and represented by Solomon and Jesus), must control the bodily faculties (represented by Satan), and not fall into temptation (Nasafi 1965: 203–4).[12]

One of the problems facing man in his battle with evil is how does his intelligence chooses between various options in any given situation? The answer is given in terms of a negative and positive definition of good conduct. Taking the negative first, good conduct means neither doing anything evil nor wishing any misfortune upon anyone. The positive definition is performing good deeds with everyone and wishing for their good-fortune. Although these definitions do not tell us what are good and evil, Nasafi states that one can recognize good and evil by their effects upon one's own soul. This is because the inner state of the person who wishes evil upon another person does not prosper but deteriorates, and the fire and torment in his own heart increase in proportion to the success and improvements of his rival's condition. In the same way, the inner state of the person who wishes well improves as the condition of his colleague prospers.[13]

Wishing evil or success upon someone is closely related to the concept of intention *(niyyat)*, since both are mental attitudes, not necessarily related to 'islam' (submission) which is the external manifestation of Islamic worship. Intention is different from an act because one person may perform an act that appears evil or contrary to God's laws, however, that person's intention may be good and in the spirit of God's laws. Nasafi highlights the problematic nature of determining the evil or goodness in intentions:

> All the religious and Islamic schools have agreed that telling lies is a terrible act of disobedience, and they have seen and spoken the truth. However, there is a time when speaking the truth is a terrible disobedience and there is a time when lying is a great act of worship. So it is clear that understanding good and evil is a difficult task.
>
> (Nasafi 1973: 251)

Many Sufis drew inspiration from the *hadith* 'the believer's intention is better than his action'.[14] Before the period when this *hadith* appeared in Sufi writings, Islamic theology had reached the pragmatic solution that membership of the community could not be determined by acts alone, for faith (which is intimately linked with intention) was also a crucial component of Islam.[15] This distinction between acts and faith may be understood by using the terminology of the Sufis. For example, faith can be seen as the meaning or reality whereas the act is the form, that is, faith is the 'non-manifest' or inner dimension, and the act is the 'manifest' or outer dimension. Nasafi portrays Sufi faith as having pure intention and high aspiration, and performing bodily asceticism and having control over the lower soul (Nasafi 1965: 129).

Nasafi does not discuss the concept of intention in great depth in his works, perhaps because of the tension between the need to obey the *shari'a* and performing actions based upon one's purpose which may contravene the *shari'a* in the short-term but ultimately conform to its general spirit. His response would probably have been that it is one's ultimate duty to respect the *shari'a* (Nasafi 1973: 285–86) and acting according to one's intention is restricted to those with a high degree of spirituality who understand the outer and inner reality of the *shari'a*.

2 EVIL IN THE MACROCOSM

The Christian Perspective

As seen in the previous section, God is revealed to humanity through Jesus, with the eyes of the head. In this sense, there is no mystical element in Irenaeus' position. However, if mysticism is the experience of the divine, then Irenaeus comes close in the following: 'Those who received and bear the Spirit of God arc led to the Word, that is to the Son. But the Son takes them up and presents them to the Father, and the Father bestows incorruptibility' (cited in Minns 1994: 47). In this respect, the Irenaean world view is exclusivist: salvation is limited to those who have accepted Christ.

However, there are also certain passages in the New Testament which appear to endorse a natural theology open to all. For example, Paul states in Romans 1:19–21, 'from the creation of the world his invisible nature, namely his eternal power and deity, are clearly perceived in the things that have been made.' This view is also adopted by Irenaeus for 'He takes it as given that the created world...is a place of wonder and delight, and deduces that it has been created by a God of infinitely rich diversity and goodness whose purpose is that his sentient and intelligent creatures should endure forever, always discovering new occasions for wonder and delight in God' (Minns 1994: 25). One likely reason that natural theology appealed to Irenaeus was because it refuted the ideas of the gnostics who held that matter was evil and the source of all corruption and decay. However, the exclusivism of salvation through Christ on the one hand, and acquiring knowledge of God through natural theology on the other hand, is not worked out. Yet it is clear that according to Irenaeus, the divine can be contemplated in both the microcosm and the macrocosm.

Even though it is the earth or the flesh that is in a state of becoming, and in the end perishes with death, Irenaeus emphasizes the resurrection of the body and spirit. This bodily resurrection is interpreted in a literal manner. Irenaeus points out that a new Jerusalem will descend upon a new earth since 'Earth and heaven will pass away,' (Matthew 26:35) and will be based upon the model of the old Jerusalem. The body of the old world was destined to perish, as 1 Cornthians 7:31 predicts, 'The fashion of this world is passing away', but when this fashion perishes 'man will be renewed for imperishability so that he can no longer grow old, and "that will be the new heaven and the earth" (Isaiah 65:17) in which the new man will dwell, conversing with God in a manner always new' (Irenaeus 1997: V, 36:1).

Irenaeus points to the scriptures that declare that humans lived beyond 700, 800, and 900 years (Irenaeus 1997: 164–5). 'It seems incredible and impossible to modern people, ignorant of God's "economies," that a man can live so many years, but our ancestors lived that long, as do those who have been translated to prefigure the future "length of days" (Psalms, 23:6; 91:16)' (Irenaeus 1997: V, 5.1). Moreover, eternal life is given to the flesh through the Eucharist of the blood and the body of Christ. This being the case, it would seem that Irenaeus could not logically hold the macrocosm to be evil, since the flesh of the microcosm is based on the earth of the macrocosm.

Although the macrocosm is not intrinsically evil, there are still questions to be answered about those events that occur in the macrocosm, such as earthquakes and other natural disasters, and the massacre of the innocent. Irenaeus does not provide explicit answers to such problems, but he does affirm that there is a purpose behind everything. God knows everything, as Matthew 10:30 states, 'The hairs of your head are all counted' (cited by Irenaeus 1997: II, 26.3): 'Absolutely nothing has been made or is being made without reason and by chance, but on the contrary everything has been made with a divine harmony and a sublime art' (Irenaeus 1997: II, 26.3). Irenaeus refers to the human inability to comprehend God's knowledge of the fall and rise of the oceans, the origin of rain, why the moon waxes and wanes, and he could also have included the occurrence of natural disasters. He states that such questions can be resolved through God's grace, but others are left to God. In this way, 'God may be always teaching and man always learning from God' (Irenaeus 1997: II, 28.3). In effect, this contributes to the overall pattern of human development. Even if someone is harmed or killed in a natural disaster, this should not be considered as evil, for as Irenaeus states, 'When the partial is destroyed these will continue: faith, hope, love' (1 Corinthians 13:9–13; Irenaeus 1997: II, 28.3).

The answer for Irenaeus lies in trust in God. The alternative is destined to fail, for human reason cannot fathom the infinite links piecing together the wisdom of all events that occur in this world. Attempts at intellectual comprehension are futile, as discovered by Ivan Karamazov, in Dostoevsky's novel *The Brothers Karamazov*, for he fell in to madness, having lost in his struggle to cope with a rational understanding of evil. (It is perhaps significant that the milieu in which Dostoevsky wrote was Greek Orthodox – an interpretation of Christianity that bears more similarity to the Irenaean position than that of the Roman Catholic church).[16]

However, the argument that natural disasters are all part of God's plan and serve as a teaching device in the development of man would do little to assuage the criticisms of the innocent victims of massacres or natural disasters. Why should small children in Africa die of starvation? No doubt they would prefer to live and learn the lessons that God gives through the suffering of children in other areas.

The Sufi Perspective

Perceiving the reality of the divine through the macrocosm was a problem for some Christians. This was because if God can be contemplated through his acts in the macrocosm, the centrality of Jesus is called in to question. Islam faces no such problems because the Qur'an confirms that all prophets delivered genuine messages, thus those who do not follow the laws revealed to Muhammad may still benefit if they obey the laws of their own messenger. Indeed, the Qur'an states that all nations were sent prophets (10:47), some of whom were unknown to Muhammad (40:78). On this basis, Islamic tradition came to accept the validity of other religions (as long as their prophets lived prior to Muhammad). Thus Islam, especially in the Sufi interpretation, is an inclusive religion. Moreover, Muslims believed that in addition to the information provided by the prophets, God could be known through contemplation of the macrocosm. Such a position was legitimized with reference to the Qur'an, which includes numerous verses advising man to contemplate the 'signs' of God in the world:

> And of His signs is that He created you of dust; then you are mortals, scattered abroad.

> And of His signs is that He created you of yourselves, spouses, that you might repose in them, and He has set between you love and mercy. Surely in that are signs for a people who consider.
> And of His signs is the creation of the heavens and earth, and the variety of your tongues and hues. Surely in that are signs for those who know.
> And of His signs is your slumbering by night and day, and your seeking after His bounty. Surely in that are signs for a people who hear.
> And of His signs, He shows you lightening, for fear and hope. He sends down water from heaven. He revives the earth after it is dead. Surely in that are signs for a people who understand.
> And of His signs is that the heaven and earth stand firm by His command; then, when he calls you once and suddenly, out of the earth, you shall come forth.
>
> (30:19–24)

> And of His signs is that He sends the winds as heralds of good tidings, giving you a taste of His mercy—that the ships may sail by His command and that you may seek His bounty, in order that you may be grateful.
>
> (30: 46)

It is interesting to note that the Arabic word for the 'signs' in the above verses is the same Arabic word that is used to refer to the verses of the Qur'an itself. God's signs, that is, His verses *(aya)* in the Qur'an, and His signs *(aya)* in the macrocosm, confirm one another.

The idea that God reveals himself through the macrocosm was presented in a unique work by Ibn Tufayl (d. 1185) a philosopher and court physician of the Spanish Almohad Sultan, Abu Yaqub Yusuf. Ibn Tufayl relates a story about a child on a desert island who has been reared by a doe. Through the use of reason, the child is able to comprehend the world around him, and as an adult he realizes that there is a cause behind everything and eventually perceives God in a mystical manner. In this way, man can know of the existence of God without scriptural revelation (Goodman 1972).

Nasafi's Sufi vision of the macrocosm is centred upon the concept that existence is one, which is the existence of God.

This being the case, it is impossible for any kind of existence to be bad or evil, whether it is Necessary Existence (that is God, the source of all existence) or contingent existence (such as man who exists through God). Belief in the perfection of all existence, including contingent existence, provoked major theological discussions prior to Nasafi's era. It was argued by Ghazali (d. 1111) that God had to create the best of all possible worlds because refraining from doing so would be an indication of miserliness, an attribute which stands in contrast to His generosity and justice. However, this argument implies the impossibility of God creating an even better world, a severe restriction on his power. These two positions reflect the conflict between the rational theologians who emphasized reason and God's justice (the *Mu'tazilites*) and the 'orthodox' theologians who stressed the primacy of God's power.

In Nasafi's system where the world is the best possible, all existents have a purpose, which is to reach their ultimate perfection. It is impossible for anything to be 'evil' so long as it performs its function, and if anything is omitted from existence in the 'chain of being', then the unity of existence and its perfection will cease. This is the concept of the plenitude in which existence appears in all its glory, from the lowest of the low to the highest of the high.[17] Even acts of creation that some humans consider 'natural disasters' have a purpose, contributing to the full manifestation of existence, but in most cases man cannot fathom the wisdom behind them. In such situations, Nasafi comments that Sufis should adopt the character traits of remaining silent *(khamush)*, being satisfied *(razi dadan)* in God and surrendering *(taslim)* to him. Man can only gaze *(nizara kardan)* at the manifestation of such divine attributes that appear incongruous to him.[18]

Nasafi discusses the plenitude as if each individual component is alive with a desire to attain its perfection and thus reveal the beauty of the whole. All individual units, from the spheres, the elements and compounds are motivated by love, desiring to reach their goal, which is man.[19] He is the perfect lover of all existent things because he is able to witness God through them all. Thus the aim of creation is reached through man, and the love and servitude of all things to man (such as the use of animals in farming and hunting, utilizing wood and stone for building) is dramatically represented in an analogy of man as the *Ka'ba* and the existent things revolving around and bowing to him:

> All existents are parts of man. All the parts of the world are working and are busy with progress and ascent until man is created at the end...So man is the *Ka'ba* of the existents because they all turn to face him. The prostration of the angels was because they were all his workers:[20] 'And He has subjected to you what the heavens and earth contain'
>
> (Qur'an 55:12).
>
> Prostration is not placing one's forehead to the ground. Rather, it is performing something for someone. All the existents prostrate to man and they do this because the Perfect Man exists among the human beings...
> ...the Perfect Man is the select and quintessence of existents...and the cherubs, spiritual beings, the Throne, the Footstool, the heavens and the planets are his servants, and they continually rotate around him, assisting in his tasks.
>
> (Nasafi 1963: 19, 11–13)

Although man is the telos of the existing things, he is dependent upon those things that are 'lower' than him in the ontological hierarchy created by God (Nasafi 1973: 266). Nasafi explains the order and hierarchy of existent things in terms of an ascent *(mi'raj)* which, as has been shown, is a theme that he returns to frequently in his theosophy:

> Know that all existents, including intelligences *('uqul)*, souls *(nufus)*, natures *(taba'i')*, heavenly spheres *(aflak)*, stars *(anjum)*, elements *('anasir)* and the three kingdoms [mineral, plant and animal] are voyaging and journeying until they reach their summit *(nihayat)* and ultimate limit. Each one has a summit and ultimate limit. The summit of each thing is when whatever is existent in *potentia* becomes existent in actuality. In other words, the grain,

> seed and embryo are existent in *potentia* and then become existent in actuality. But the ultimate limit of each thing is when it reaches man. When they reach man, the ascent *(mi'raj)* of all existent things is completed. So the ascent is in this manner and the Messenger was correct when he said, 'Last night I ascended and reached the Throne and saw God.'
>
> (Nasafi 1965: 144–5)[21]

The unity and multiplicity within the plenitude are portrayed by Nasafi through another analogy which highlights the order and servitude of the existent things in their relationship with man. He describes existents as a single tree, for the sphere of spheres (or the Throne) is the ground of the tree, the second sphere (or the Footstool) is the root, and the seven heavens are the tree-trunk. The fourfold elements and natures are the branches of the tree, while the minerals, plants and animals are the leaves, flowers and fruit of the tree, and man is the fruit of the tree.

Nasafi attempts to explain the evil of natural disasters and massacres, with reference to the idea of the unity of existence. The full manifestation of existence is the aim of creation, and as already mentioned above, this is witnessed through the macrocosm and the microcosm. Such a full manifestation of existence means that all of the divine attributes must be displayed, not only love and kindness, but also wrath and anger. Nasafi describes existence as light that shines through the niches of the genera and species of the world. Sometimes there are many niches and at other times there are few niches. When there is one niche for a particular attribute, the light shining from it becomes very strong, as opposed to when the light is diffused among many niches and becomes weak. So when there is only one niche for an attribute, this niche is a leader or chief. He may be a leader in kindness or in anger and mass killing (Nasafi 1985: 81), thus individuals as different as Jesus and Chingiz Khan are instruments by which God manifests Himself.

A similar idea to Nasafi's was discussed by Ibn 'Arabi who explained the slaughter of young boys in Egypt when Moses and the Jews were prevented from leaving Egypt (Exodus 11). As a result of this killing, the strength (or light) of each child killed reverted to Moses, bestowing him with more strength (Austin 1980: 251–52). Thus Moses became the Perfect Man to manifest the divine attributes. The suffering and evil inflicted upon the boys was for the eventual benefit of the world as a whole, and in this way God's wrath and anger may also be seen in terms of His love and kindness.

Yet again, the obvious problem remains that the innocent victims, one assumes, would find it difficult to accept such an explanation of evil. Islamic theologians from a very early period had addressed this issue and failed to reach an adequate solution. By the ninth century, the problem of evil was discussed through a story of three brothers. The first reached maturity and embraced Islam, and so went to Heaven when he died. The second, on maturity, was an unbeliever and so was cast into Hell when he died. The third, however, died while still an infant and was placed in limbo. Since Heaven is the reward for those who perform worthy deeds and obey God, it follows that the child cannot gain entry to Heaven because children are not culpable before the law, as mentioned earlier. It might be argued that God had the child killed at an early age because He knew that the child would become wicked as an adult. This would naturally cause the second wicked brother to ask why God did not kill him at an early age and thus avoid Hell (Watt 1948: 136–7).

CONCLUSION

Although neither Irenaeus nor Nasafi were able to provide watertight theodicies, their world views depicted man in a positive light. In both systems although sin is disobedience to God, it is necessarily permitted because it leads man back to him. The path of redemption for the Christian sinner is through Jesus. He is the model of perfected humanity, by which individuals can approach perfection, or, the likeness of God.

After Jesus ascended to heaven, man can maintain a link with this perfection through the Holy Spirit. The possibility of achieving perfection never vanishes, and the connection with the divine is never broken. Irenaeus argues his point with reference to 1 Corinthians: 'To each is given the manifestation of the Spirit for his benefit.' Sin also leads back to God for Muslims, for once conscious of sin the believer has the opportunity to repent as *sura* 39:53 states: 'Say: 'My servants, those who have gone beyond the limits, do not despair of Allah's mercy, for He forgives all sins. Truly He is all-forgiving and all-merciful.' Moreover, God always provides examples for sinners by which they can learn the path to perfection. Nasafi states that the prophets were sinless, and after the sealing of prophecy with Muhammad, the Friends of God are also sinless (Nasafi 1965: 116–8). Moreover, there always exists a Perfect Man in the world; he is like the world's heart. His purpose is to maintain the link between God and man, and the Resurrection will occur when the Perfect Man no longer exists in the world (Ridgeon 1998a: 176).

Likewise, the appearance of evil in the macrocosm is a manifestation of His power (and understood by some Sufis in utilitarian terms as a manifestation of kindness). Yet for most people the reasons for natural disasters, from a theistic perspective, are unjustifiable. Therefore, both Christians and Muslims advise believers that the best policy is to trust God. Moreover, natural disasters may even have the benefit of assisting in human development or progress by strengthening the 'mystery of faith'. Rumi, who fled from the terrors perpetrated by the Mongols, was well aware of the difficulty in realizing the existence of the divine when there appeared to be so many disasters and so much distress in the world, and the following is his advice:

> Don't look at these events of Time which come from heaven and are unpalatable here.
> Don't look at the lamentation over daily bread and means of livelihood. Don't look at this drought, this fear, this trembling.

Look at this! Despite all the world's bitterness, you are [still] mortally attached to it and its heedless occupant.
Consider the bitter trials to be a mercy! ...
Were there no bitter command [from God], were there no good and evil, no rock or pearl,
Were there no lower self, Satan or sensuality; were there no wound, war or weeping,
Then O profane man! By what name or title would the king call his own servants?
How could he say 'O patient one' or 'O forbearing one'? How could he say, 'O brave one' or 'O wise one'?
How could there be patient, sincere and generous men without highwaymen or the accursed Devil?
The tyranny of Time and each torment are lighter to bear than distance from the Truth and forgetting [Him].
The former pass away, but the latter abide. Fortune lies with he who carries a spirit aware [of Him].

(Rumi 1925–40: VI, 1733–57)

NOTES

1. A more Islamic version of this article appeared in Ridgeon 1998b.
2. Shaykh Fadlallah was the spiritual mentor of Hizbullah.
3. The Qur'anic portrayal of Adam's fall appears in 20:118–22.
4. Najm al-Din Kubra (d. 1220) cites a *hadith* that permits a sinner entry to heaven even though he had performed no good acts except uttering the Islamic testament of faith. See Najm al-Din Kubra 1361: 33–34.

   ...that day when the servant is brought forward on the day of resurrection, his good deeds and bad deeds will be measured in the arena of the resurrection. His bad deeds will [weigh] very much in the scales, [and] the Truth Most High will say, 'Don't you have any good deeds?' He will say, 'O God, I don't have any, ' and he will despair of his own situation. Then God Most High will say, 'There is one good deed with Us. Once you said, 'There is no god but God'.' That utterance of the testimony of faith will be brought forth and it will be written on a piece of paper that amounts to no more than a nail. This servant will see the many ranks of his own bad acts, and then he will see that paper which amounts to no more than a nail. He will say, 'O God! What is the value of this one nail next to those registers of bad deeds?' The Truth Most High will say, 'There is no injustice today.' This piece of paper that amounts to one nail will be placed in one pan of the scales and the register of bad deeds will be placed in the other pan. [The pan with] the register of bad deeds will suddenly shoot upwards, and the pan of 'there is no god but God' will be very heavy. Thus [the servant] will be taken to heaven.

5. Genesis 2:5–6. The earth that God used to mould Adam had not been rained upon, nor had it been tilled.
6. Qur'an, 36:82, 'His command, when He desires a thing, is to say to it 'Be!' and it is.'
7. According to Islamic tradition, the snake, peacock, Satan and Eve all played a part in Adam's temptation. Iblis could not enter Paradise to tempt Adam because he was not given permission to enter. He told the peacock that its beauty would pass away unless it ate from the tree of immortality. Iblis said that he could show the peacock where this tree was if he could enter Paradise. Because of the peacock's pride in its beauty, it wanted to help Iblis, so it fetched the snake. Iblis transformed himself into the wind and hid himself in the snake's mouth. In this way Iblis entered Paradise and was able to tempt Adam. *See*, Awn 1983: 42–43. Nasafi makes a distinction between Iblis and Satan in his discussion of the microcosm. He states that Adam is the spirit, Eve is the body, Satan is nature *(tabi'at)*, Iblis is the faculty of sensory intuition *(wahm)*, the peacock is man's appetites *(shahwat)* and the snake is the faculty of force *(ghasb)*, *see*, Nasafi 1963: 22, 17.
8. Nasafi, *Kitab-i tanzil*, fol. 75a, lines 1–5.
9. Muslims believe that *sura* 17:1 of the Qur'an refers to this night journey: 'Glory to the One who took his servant on a night journey from the sacred place of prayer [Mecca] to the furthest place of prayer [Jerusalem].'
10. Qur'an, 2:29, 'It is He who created for you all that is in the earth, then He lifted Himself to heaven and levelled them seven heavens; and He has knowledge of everything.'
11. Qur'an, 2:254, 'His Footstool embraces the heavens and earth,' and Qur'an, 20:5, 'The Merciful Who is established upon the Throne.'
12. *Ibid.*, 10:18.
13. It is interesting that Dostoevsky 1985: 37, makes a similar point in *The House of the Dead*:
    Nearly all the convicts talked and raved in their sleep at night. Oaths, underworld slang, knives and axes figured most prominently in their ravings. 'We're beaten men,' this used to say, 'we've had the insides beaten out of us, that's why we cry out at night.'
14. For example, *see*, Hujwiri 1976: 4, and Suhrawardi 1973: 97.
15. For the early development of Islamic theology and the problems surrounding acts and faith see Watt 1962. The *Kharijites* held that the sinner could not be a member of their community and it was legitimate

to kill the sinner. In a reaction to this, the *Murji'ites* believed that only God could judge people's sins, thus they stressed faith as a condition of membership of the community.

16. 'The basic Irenaean conception of man as a creature made initially in the 'image' of God and gradually being brought through his own free responses into the divine 'likeness', this creative process being interrupted by the fall and set right again by the incarnation, has continued to operate in the minds of the theologians of the Orthodox Church to the present day,' (Hick 1996: 223).
17. The principle of the plenitude was not an original argument, for Ghazali had discussed it prior to Nasafi, see Ormsby 1984: 198.
18. Nasafi, *Kitab-i tanzil*, C112, fol. 80b, lines 13–14.
19. *Ibid.*, fol. 73a, lines 16–19.
20. The prostration of the angels to man occurs in the Qur'an, 2:31.
21. For Nasafi, man has his own *mi'raj* within the self; the Throne is the heart of the believer. He cites a *hadith* which states 'the heart of the believer is the throne of God Almighty,' (Nasafi 1963: 237). Once the tarnishing of the world has been polished off the heart, its rightful owner, intelligence, which is God's deputy (Nasafi 1985: 110) can be firmly established upon it. Thus the Perfect Man represents how God is master of his creation.

4

Jihad: Christianity under Threat or in Defence of Islam?

The mosques are our barracks, the domes our helmets,
the minarets our bayonets, and the faithful are our soldiers.[1]

In December 1997, the quatrain of Turkish poetry given above, was recited publicly by Tayyip Erdogan, mayor of Istanbul, and subsequently he received a jail sentence of ten months. In his defence, the mayor stated that the poem represented an appeal for peace, presumably meaning that *jihad* is confined to the mosques as merely a spiritual *jihad*. The Turkish special state security court did not share the same opinion, and found him guilty of 'inciting hatred.'[2]

Differences in the interpretation of *jihad* are not a recent phenomenon, for *jihad* has existed since the inception of Islam in the seventh century. Yet in the present age, the initial image that the average western person has of *jihad* would probably reflect the views of the Turkish security court. *Jihad*, turmoil in the Middle East, in the Gulf or in the Islamic Asian world, and the 'Islamic nuclear bomb' are all topics that appear regularly in the media. Yet the media is indeed justified in discussing *jihad* because there have been so many examples in recent years, some of which are more palatable to the western world than others. A short list could include the *jihad* against Israel declared by Hafiz Assad, the secular President of Syria in 1973; the *jihad* of the Afghani *mujahidin* against the Soviet Union from 1979 until the Soviet withdrawal; the *jihad* declared by Saddam Husayn during the Gulf War against Kuwait; the *fatwa* for *jihad* obtained by King Fahd of Saudi Arabia from the religious authorities against Saddam Husayn in the same war; the *jihad* against the self and its worldly desires as re-advocated by Ayatollah Khomeini during the early years of the Islamic revolution in Iran; the *jihad* of an organization named *Islamic Jihad* (associated with Hizbullah) which was connected with the suicide operations against western institutions in Lebanon during 1983; the *jihad* of the Islamic regime in Sudan under ʻUmar al-Bashir against the ʻrebels' in the south of that country, a *jihad* which contributed to the famine of 1998.

The need to understand the concept of *jihad* is as great as ever. A comprehensive survey of this topic should include an analysis of its development from its origin in the Qur'an, to the explanation of the Sufis, the expositions of the Sunni and Shiʻ-ite jurists of the classical period, and finally to the interpretations offered by nineteenth and twentieth century thinkers. It would be possible to provide a study from any one of these standpoints, however, the aim of this chapter is to present an introduction to *jihad* which offers a taste of the various transformations that it has undergone.

1 *JIHAD* AS FIGHTING IN EARLY ISLAM

The revelations that Muhammad believed he had received from God provoked the anger of non-believing Meccan citizens in a number of ways. In *sura* 4:75, the Qur'an accused them of ignoring the rights of the weak, the sick, the poor and orphans, all individuals who had been protected by the tribal chiefs in previous generations, but were now ignored by the newly emerging urban élite. Moreover, the Qur'an denounced Meccan polytheistic beliefs and practices centred at the *Kaʻba.* The wealthy merchants must have considered this as a threat to their position since the *Kaʻba* generated much income as it was a site of pilgrimage. Therefore, Muhammad was not merely shunned, but fiercely opposed by non-Muslims, and he was forced to seek the protection offered from the inhabitants of a nearby city that came to be known as Medina. Yet the security of his community was somewhat tenuous, for he still faced strong opposition from the Meccans, and in addition he could not rely on the economic support of the Medinans. It was necessary for the Muslims to fortify their own position, and some Muslims did this by engaging in raids against the Meccan trade caravans that travelled back and forth to Syria. This policy of attacking trade caravans or neighbouring tribes had been a standard practice among the nomads of Arabia in the generations preceding Muhammad's era, indeed, it has been called their 'national sport' in which loss of life was infrequent (Watt 1976: 141). Yet these raids were legitimised by the Qur'an:

> Permission is given to those who fight *(yuqatalun)* because they are wronged—surely God is capable of giving them victory–those who were driven out of their homes unjustly, merely for their saying, 'Our Lord is God.' Had God not repelled some people by others, surely monasteries, churches, synagogues and mosques, wherein the name of God is mentioned frequently, would have been demolished.
>
> (22:39–40)

> They will question you concerning the holy month and fighting in it. Say: 'Fighting in it is a heinous thing, but to bar from God's way—and disbelief in Him—and the holy mosque, and to expel its people from it, that is more heinous in God's sight. And persecution is more heinous than slaying.'
>
> (2:217)

The imperative for *jihad*, as Sachedina has indicated (1988: 106) 'represents a basic moral requirement to protect the well-being of a community'. It was a means to eradicate 'corruption on earth' and to 'enjoin the good and forbid the evil'. As Muhammad's community expanded, new revelations from God permitted fighting only to those who had come from Mecca to Medina, (16:110–11) but when under attack from the Meccans, all Muslims including those who had joined the community at a later stage were obliged to fight to defend Medina (2:186–90). However, the fighting was not considered a war of aggression, it was defensive:

> And fight in the way of God with those that fight you, but aggress not: God loves not the aggressors.
>
> (2:190)

The fighting was not always popular among the Muslim community:

> Prescribed for you is fighting, although it is hateful to you. Yet it is possible you will hate a thing which is better for you; and it is possible that you will love a thing which is worse for you. God knows and you know not.
>
> (2:216)

Some of those who had joined Muhammad in Medina still had family members in Mecca, and this meant that there was a possibility of fighting against them. However, the Qur'an stressed that the most important tie among humans was of religion and not blood, therefore it was necessary to fight in God's way:

> Say: 'If it is your fathers, sons, brothers, wives, tribe, wealth that you have gained, and the commerce that for which you fear decline, and dwellings which you love more than God and His messenger and *jihad* in His way, then wait until God brings about His command. God does not guide the wrongdoing tribe.'
>
> (9:24)

Comfort was given to those who feared death through engaging in *jihad*:

> And do not think those who have been killed in the way of God as dead; they are rather living with their Lord, well provided for.
>
> (3:169)

The *hadith* literature elaborated on this Qur'anic verse; the spirits of the dead were placed in the bodies of green birds that fly around Paradise, drinking of its rivers and eating its fruits, resting upon lamps of gold under the shade of God's throne (Ayoub 1992: 218). Islamic tradition held that martyrs entered heaven without an examination of any of their worldly deeds. It has been reported that the 'suicide-bombers' of the present age prepared themselves for death by performing ritual ablutions, adorning themselves with henna and perfumes so that the angels could receive them (Partner 1997: 51).

Another incentive to participate in *jihad* was the belief that Muslims were not fighting alone, for God was with them in their battles. In a decisive victory over the Meccans at Badr, *sura* 8:17 states that it was God that slew the Meccans, not the Muslims. Indeed, the importance of *jihad* to the Islamic community is demonstrated in the early *hadith* literature, for in some traditions *jihad* is considered as one of the pillars of Islam (Ayoub 1992: 217).

Although it has been argued by some scholars that *jihad* is primarily defensive, other scholars have indicated that *jihad* can be for offensive purposes since the aim of Islam is to create a world order of believers. The universality of Islam, as the perfected religion that supersedes all others, is seen by some Muslims in the following verse:

> Today I have perfected My religion for you, and I have completed My blessing upon you, and I have approved Islam for your religion.
>
> (5:3)

This verse was revealed at the so-called 'Farewell Pilgrimage' towards the end of Muhammad's life, and tradition has affirmed that this legitimises the universality and superiority of Islam. Other verses in the Qur'an can be read in such a manner that confirm the supremacy of Islam over all other religions:

> It is He who sent His messenger with the guidance and the religion of the truth, in order to make it triumph over religion, all of it, even if the Associators should resent it.
>
> (9:33)

However the translation of the above verse into English is very difficult because it is ambiguous in the Arabic. The problem centres on the phrase 'all of it'. As mentioned above, the verse may be understood as endorsing a triumph over all religions. However, it is also possible to interpret it in the way of Mahmud Shaltut (whose thought is discussed later) who understands the verse as a triumph of individual religion, 'so that people obtain religious freedom and are not oppressed or tortured because of their religion' (cited in R. Peters 1996: 74). And again, the following verse has the same structure as the previous one, and can be interpreted either way:

> And fight them, so that sedition might end and religion, all of it, will be that of God. Then if they desist, God is fully aware of what they do.
>
> (8:39)

Of course the problem of understanding *jihad* as offensive or defensive concerns Jews and Christians, also called the 'People of the Book' who are described with respect in some verses and with hostility in others. The outcome was that they were assigned a special status, and were called *dhimmis*, permitted to live within the Islamic community on the basis of the following revelation:

> Fight those among the People of the Book who do not believe in God and the Last Day, do not forbid what God and His messenger have forbidden, and do not profess the true religion, till they pay the poll-tax out of hand and submissively.
>
> (9:29)

The *dhimmis* were so named because *dhimma* 'means a compact, which the believer agrees to respect, the violation of which makes him liable to *dhamm* (blame)' (Khadduri 1979: 176–7). On paying the tribute (referred to in the previous Qur'anic verse) which came to be known as the *jizyah*, the *dhimmis* were guaranteed protection. The *hadith* literature offered guidelines on the relationship between *jihad* and how non-Muslims could become *dhimmis*:

> When you meet your enemies among the Associators, offer them three choices. Whichever of these they agree to, accept it from them and cease hostilities against them.
> [First] call them to Islam, and if they accept your call, you too must receive them well and make peace with them...
> [Second] if they refuse, then demand that they pay the *jizyah*, and if they agree, accept it from them.
> [Third] if they still refuse, then ask God's help against them and fight against them.
>
> (Ayoub 1992: 227–8)

The non-Muslims who agreed to pay the *jizyah* became members of the community, but they did not have to participate in the *jihad*, although there were certain occasions and qualification according to which they could join the defense of the community (Khadduri 1979: 178). The opportunity to make the religion 'that of God' through *jihad*, or at least to absorb a large number of *dhimmis* into the Islamic community increased as a result of the warfare between the Byzantine and Sassanian empires. The struggle for supremacy between these two superpowers left them both exhausted, and North Africa, the Levant and Iran remained defenceless against the Muslim forces whose primary aim, according to Watt, was material gain (Watt 1976 147). This desire caused 'Umar, the second caliph, to forbid the men of Muhammad's tribe to leave Medina for the *jihad.* He is reported to have said: 'I shall catch the men of Quraysh by the throat at the entrances of this city, so that they will not be able to leave' (Ayoub 1992: 219). Yet it was 'Umar himself who instituted the practice of paying a stipend to those who participated in the *jihad*. This became a financial burden to the nascent Islamic state since *jihad* brought about conversion to Islam and the converts themselves then became eligible to engage in *jihad* and claim their reward. This resulted in discouraging conversion to Islam, it was even forbidden for a short period of time after 700 (Watt 1976: 149).

There is a certain ambiguity then concerning the concept of *jihad* during the life of Muhammad. At the beginning of his calling, it certainly seems that *jihad* was a defensive action, but as the community expanded through Arabia he sought to include many of the outlying tribes, some of which were Christian. Indeed, during the expedition to Tarbuk towards the end of his life, Muhammad sought the submission from Christian tribes that were within recognized Syrian territory. However, to regard Muhammad as merely seeking material wealth and glory surely misses the essence of the Islamic message of social reform and spiritual welfare, which he desired to implant among mankind. One modern scholar has made the following analogy: 'In modern terms the difference between Muhammad and Jesus was the difference between Nelson Mandela and Mahatma Ghandi' (Partner 1997: 35).

2 *JIHAD* AS PIETY AND THE SUFI PERSPECTIVE

The discussion so far has focused entirely upon *jihad* as a concept related to fighting, however, another vital dimension of *jihad* is referred to in the Qur'an and *hadith*. One very famous *hadith* refers to two dimensions of *jihad*. When returning from battle against the enemies of Islam, Muhammad is reported to have said: 'We have returned from the Lesser *jihad* to the Greater *jihad*.' On being asked, 'What is the Greater *jihad*?' he replied 'It is the struggle against one's self' (Furuzanfar 1982: no. 34). Sufyan ibn 'Uyayna, a Sufi who lived over a hundred and eighty years after Muhammad, referred to the above *hadith* when he stated that the *jihad* in the way of God consists of ten parts. Only one is fighting against the enemy while the other nine are fighting against the self (Watt 1976: 155). The Qur'an, in fact, testifies indirectly to the need to struggle against one's own soul:

> And strive *(jahidu)* for God as you ought to strive. He elected you, and did not impose on you any hardship in religion...
> So perform the prayer, and pay the alms, and hold fast to God.
> (22:78)

In addition, some Sufis referred to *sura* 26:69: 'And those who strive *(jahadu)* in Our cause We shall guide them in Our ways', believing that those who strove would contemplate God – the highest reward possible for man (Hujwiri 1976: 200–202). In the formative period of Islam when concepts of piety were developing within Sufism, there was also a proliferation in the collection of *hadith*. Some scholars compiled books of *hadith* devoted entirely to *jihad*, the earliest of which is that of al-Mubarak (d. 797). The vague nature of some of the *hadith* permits interpretations that support either the spiritual or military *jihad*:

> Every community has its form of monasticism, and the monasticism of this community is *jihad* in the way of God.
>
> (Ayoub 1992: 215)

> What has happened to people that they have prohibited for themselves women, good food, perfumes, sleep and the pleasures of the world, whereas I [Muhammad] have not taught you to become monks and priests. In my religion there is neither abstention from women nor from meat, neither seclusion nor withdrawal. For the purposes of self-control my religion has fasting. As for monasticism, all its benefits can be derived from *jihad*...
> Those who were destroyed before you were destroyed because they were severe with themselves, and when they became severe with themselves God became severe with them as well. It is the remnants of such people who you see in the oratories and hermitages of monks.
>
> (Ibn Kathir 1981: 626–9)

The dual nature of *jihad*, spiritual and military, is reflected in the lives of Sufis from the early period of Islamic mysticism. Some Sufis were actively engaged in physical combat with the non-Muslim enemy, for example, an early Sufi, Ibrahim Adham (d. 776 or 790) died of a wound received in battle. Sulami (936–1021) offers a more explicit connection between the spiritual struggle with the self and with the non-Muslim. He refers to the *ribat*, a Qur'anic term (8:60; 4:102) which came to mean a fortified frontier post from where *jihad* was carried out. (By the mid-ninth century, *ribats* were littered throughout Central Asia and North Africa). In Sulami's words: 'Staying in a *ribat* and battling is the best [form] of calm because when the servant becomes tired of worship to God he can engage in something else in which there is no sin,' (Sulami 1953: 101) in other words, in fighting the infidel. As Islam spread into previously non-Islamic territory, the *ribats* kept their Sufi associations since many of them were transformed into Sufi convents, which are known in Persian as *khanaqah* (Kiyani: 1990: 76).

Indeed, Sufism should not be considered as an other-worldly movement that has no concern for the day to day affairs of the world. Being a Sufi meant that one aimed for perfection, which requires one to live in, support and defend the community. A good example of this is the thirteenth century Sufi master Najm al-Din Kubra, for it is related that despite being offered protection by the invading Mongol hordes, he took up his sword and earned a martyr's death in 1221 when he was probably an octogenarian (Waley 1991: 82).

However, many Sufis emphasized the priority of the spiritual *jihad*. The Greater *jihad* was frequently discussed under the related term *mujahada*, or spiritual effort. Hujwiri (d. 1063) classified the Sufis into eleven sects, and one of these he called the Sahlis, after Sahl al-Tustari (d. 896). Hujwiri stated that all Sufis observe *mujahada*, but the Sahlis carry it to an extreme. According to the Sahlis, the spirit is controlled by intelligence whereas the lower soul is controlled by man's passions *(hawa)*, the problem being that intelligence and passion want to go in opposite directions. It is necessary therefore to obey the call of intelligence and control the lower self and passion for they are, in reality, the devil, and Hujwiri cites a *hadith* to make his point: 'Your worst enemy is between your two sides.' Since the lower soul cannot be completely destroyed, man can only obtain knowledge of it and thereby realize how it can be disciplined and controlled (Hujwiri 1976: 195–210). Hujwiri does not explain the specific methods of discipline practised by the Sahlis.

However, it is reported that Sahl al-Tustari himself taught seven major principles: 'cleaving to the book of God, following the example of the Prophet, eating lawful food, desisting from wrongdoing, avoiding sins, repentance and pursuit of God's rights' (Bowering 1980: 78).

In the medieval period, the dual nature of *jihad*, the Greater and Lesser *jihad*, was also described in many passages in Rumi's poetry. His efforts to demonstrate the superiority of Islam over Christianity resulted in several verses in which the Lesser, or military *jihad* is emphasized (as is shown in a previous chapter). However, he also had much to say about the Greater *jihad* that is described thus: 'The Prophets and Friends of God do not avoid spiritual combat. The first spiritual combat they undertake in their quest is the killing of the ego and the abandonment of personal wishes and desires. This is the Greater *jihad*' (Chittick 1983: 154).

The Sufi interiorisation of *jihad* is also shown in the writings of 'Aziz Nasafi who cited an Arabic source he called the scripture of Abraham, which portrays a pre-Muhammadan version of the five pillars:

> Silence about vain things is fasting.
> Not placing hope in the created beings is ritual prayer.
> Protection of the bodily organs is worship.
> Renunciation of caprice is *jihad*.
> Abstention from evil is the alms tax.
>
> (Nasafi 1973: 246–7)

3 CLASSICAL INTERPRETATIONS OF *JIHAD*

The Sunni Interpretation

With the death of Muhammad, the majority of Muslims recognized Abu Bakr as the deputy of God's Messenger, or Caliph and he inherited the authority to legitimize *jihad*, and subsequent caliphs also claimed such authority. The remarkable expansion of Islam in the years after Muhammad's death may be attributed to various factors, one of these was the material gain to be had through *jihad*. (However, the Qur'anic imperative to wage the military *jihad* was, no doubt, interpreted by some Muslims in such a manner that supported the goal of establishing Islam throughout the world). In addition to Qur'anic commands, the Caliphs legitimized *jihad* by referring to the actions of and stories related about Muhammad. For example, Islamic tradition holds that Muhammad sent letters to the rulers of Byzantium, Egypt, Persia and Ethiopia inviting them to accept Islam.[3] Moreover, Muhammad's last military adventure was to Tarbuk, which lay on the Gulf of Akaba, on the road to Syria. It is reported that he assembled 30,000 men, and insisted that all Muslims who were able should participate in this expedition. With this huge army, Muhammad 'was more or less aware that he was launching the Islamic state on a challenge to the Byzantine empire' (Watt 1961: 219).

The Sunni tradition emerged by following the example that they believed had been set by Muhammad. These examples were written down by scholars of the early Islamic era, and they concentrated upon his military campaigns (this is the so-called *maghazi* literature) and twenty-seven major raids were attributed to him (Partner 1997: 35). The desire to emulate Muhammad meant that Muslims were encouraged to be obedient to his caliphs. Just as Muslims assembled for *jihad* when called by Muhammad, so too they should be ready for *jihad* when proclaimed by the caliph. One Muslim scholar, al-Shaybani (d. 805) cited a tradition that confirmed the practice of *jihad* as exercised by Muhammad and the early caliphs:

> God gave the Prophet Muhammad four swords [for fighting the unbelievers]: the first against the polytheists, which Muhammad himself fought with; the second against apostates which Caliph Abu Bakr fought with; the third against the People of the Book, which Caliph 'Umar fought with; the fourth against dissenters which Caliph 'Ali fought with.
>
> (Cited in Khadduri 1979: 74)

The rapid expansion of Islam pushed the frontiers of its empire as far as India in the east and Morocco in the west. In fact the Islamic armies were prevented from gaining an entry into Europe following a defeat in 732 at Poitiers in France. When the expansion slowed down and stopped, the Islamic jurists adopted a more cautious approach in their treatises on *jihad* (Ayoub 1992: 224). Indeed, there was the precedent of a temporary truce with the Byzantines in 661 and in 678 when the Muslims had to pay an annual tribute. This resulted in the tradition that *jihad* should be waged only when the chances of success were high (Partner 1997: 48). Guidelines were established for both moral conduct when engaged in war, and also for deciding who should actually participate in *jihad*. For offensive *jihad*, or *jihad* against the *dar al-harb*, the caliph assembled an army from those who were able to fight since it was a collective duty. Exemption from this *jihad* was given to those in debt, those who were the only sons of a family, the sick and those without a horse or arms. To a large extent, this meant that the caliph had to rely on professional armies. Tradition commanded that the Islamic forces engage in *jihad* once every year (Lambton 1981: 209). With regard to the defensive *jihad*, however, it was a duty of each and every Muslim to participate.

The Shi'-ite Interpretation

The Shi'-ite understanding of *jihad* was initially somewhat different from that of the Sunnis. This was because of the very nature of Shi'-ism itself which rejects the legitimacy of the first three caliphs. Instead of recognising Abu Bakr as Muhammad's successor, Shi'-ites claim that the prophet's cousin and son-in-law, 'Ali, was designated as the leader of the community. After 'Ali, this leadership passed on through a succession of individuals known as *imams*. Each *imam* designated a successor, and each one was regarded as infallible and possessing esoteric knowledge. According to twelver-Shi'-ite belief, the twelfth *imam* disappeared, entering a stage known as the 'occultation', during which time he is present, but absent from human eyes, and he will re-appear to install a brief period of justice before the day of resurrection. The significant point, however, is that Shi'-ites believe that only the *imam* has the authority to launch a *jihad* because an offensive *jihad* can be initiated only by a just ruler 'in order to usher in the ethico-social order that the Qur'an requires' (Sachedina 1988: 109). It is the function of the imam alone, because only he has the esoteric knowledge to know what is just or unjust. With the occultation of the twelfth *imam*, a legitimate, offensive *jihad* is therefore impossible, but the defensive *jihad* is permissible. Of course word play and doublespeak can transform an offensive *jihad* into a defensive *jihad*; an enemy can be perceived to be preparing all kinds of plots for attack, and this justifies a pre-emptive attack to defend the *dar al-islam*. These arguments were refined and discussed by Shi'-ite jurists such as al-Tusi and al-Mufid during the medieval period.

In the modern period (that is, since the beginning of the nineteenth century), the Shi'-ite clerics in Iran have played a major role in politics. They have issued *fatwas* legitimizing *jihad* on several occasions, without being pressured to do so by monarchs, such as the case during the 1820s when Iran was led into war against Russia at the instigation of the religious scholars.[4] Indeed, some nineteenth century clerics even went so far as to affirm the legitimacy of an offensive *jihad* even during the occultation of the twelfth *imam* (Kohlberg 1976: 83–4). This was a result of the increasing power of the Shi-'ite clerics with the fall of the Safavid dynasty and the emergence of the Qajars who lacked any religious legitimacy to rule and sought support from the clerics.

A more traditional form of Shi-'ite *jihad* was encouraged in the 1960s in a series of lectures given by Ayatollah Mutahhari (Lawrence 1998: 175–81). He affirmed that the only legitimate form of *jihad* was defensive, and could only be waged against soldiers on the battlefield. Mutahhari stated that non-Muslims could participate in such a *jihad* because the ultimate form of *jihad* is that in defence of any group fighting for freedom of belief, or freedom of thought which are the universal rights of humanity. He cites the example of non-Muslims fighting with Algerians against the French. From Mutahhari's interpretation, defensive *jihad* is to preserve freedom of belief, therefore can one conclude that a Christian *jihad* and a secular *jihad* are legitimate? If this is the case, then in all probability the *dar al-islam* and the *dar al-harb* will continue to co-exist, and this makes sense from a traditional Shi-'ite perspective because justice will only be restored to the world when the *imam*, or *Mahdi* returns.

The Islamic revolution of 1978 continued the process of re-thinking Islam and therefore of *jihad*, and the revolutionaries justified their actions as the defence of Islam. If the historical circumstances of twentieth century Iran are taken into consideration it is possible to comprehend the claim that the actions taken by the Islamic Republic are purely defensive. (Such circumstances include the CIA-backed overthrow of Musaddiq, the democratically elected Prime Minister in 1953, and the excesses of Muhammad Reza Pahlavi's regime, especially from 1963 until his downfall in 1978).

The Islamic nature of the revolution and defence of Islam were themes that were continually repeated by Ayatollah Khomeini. He criticized those religious clerics who refrained from any political involvement, merely hoping that the twelfth *imam* would reappear to restore justice and lead the *jihad*. According to Khomeini, this kind of belief is erroneous because it avoids the responsibility of the Shi'-ite religious clerics to form a government (Khomeini 1985: 220). This means 'equipping and mobilizing armies, appointing governors and officials, levying taxes and expending them for the welfare of a particular person' (*Ibid*.: 62). Yet all of this is in defence of Islam, to replace the un-Islamic system that was both directly and indirectly foisted upon Iran. Khomeini accused the imperialists of keeping the Iranians weak through propaganda and exploiting all Iranian resources. Moreover, foreigners and their agents (that is, the Pahlavi monarchs) had cast aside Islamic laws and replaced them with European laws and institutions

(*Ibid.*: 34–5). After the revolution of 1978, the Islamic regime was able to implement its defensive *jihad* against the imperialists. Two of the most famous slogans to come out of the Islamic Republic of Iran are 'neither East nor West, only the Islamic Republic' (Ramazani 1988: 21), and 'America is worse than Britain, Britain is worse than America. The Soviet Union is worse than both of them. They are all worse and more unclean than each other' (Bernard & Khalilzad 1985: 151–2). The sense of frustration, bitterness and helplessness of an exploited and weak people screams out from every word in this kind of polemic. In more comprehensible language Khomeini stated:

> How much you talk about the West, claiming that we must measure Islam in accordance with Western criteria! What an error! In gratitude for the bounty of liberty you have received, you should be loyal to Islam.
>
> (Khomeini 1985: 272)

Fred Halliday, a contemporary specialist on Iran has stated: 'Ayatollah Khomeini's rhetoric was not one calling for *jihad* to conquer or convert the non-Muslim world, but was a cry of concern: "Islam is in danger" *(islam dar khatar)*' (Halliday 1996: 120).

Khomeini equated the return to Islam with the Greater *jihad*, or the *jihad* against the self. His defence of Islam was the preservation of a way of life that continues in Iran in many forms, even after his death, such as the recent attempts to restrict the satellite broadcasts of *Baywatch* starring Pamela Anderson. But is it really possible to regard the policies of Iran under Khomeini as solely defensive? Not all Iranians or western academics have regarded Khomeini's actions as a defensive response (Lawrence 1998: 179–82). There are three issues which highlight the problematic nature of determining the defensive or offensive attitude: the continuation of the war with Iraq; the export of the revolution; the Salman Rushdie affair.

One of the reasons that may have caused the secular Sunni Iraqi regime to initiate the military war with Iran was its worry that the Iranian revolution would have an effect on the Iraqi Shi'-ite population. The Iranian re-action to the Iraqi attack was largely expressed in terms of the defence of Islam (Ramazani 1988: 25, 64; Lawrence 1998: 178), and Khomeini did not appear to invoke Muslims for *jihad* (Partner 1997: 247). However, claims about 'the defence of Islam' were called into question when Iraq seemed willing to halt the fighting but Khomeini remained intransigent, despite the sacrifice of thousands of Iranian soldiers. He was finally persuaded to drink the 'chalice of poison' and accept a ceasefire after eight years.

Secondly, after the revolution there were suspicions that Iran was involved in various intrigues in Lebanon, the Gulf states and Saudi Arabia to further its export of the revolution. The Lebanese connection was more explicit than anywhere else, for a thousand Iranian Revolutionary Guards joined forces with radical Shi'-ite Lebanese in the Bekaa Valley, who became known as Hizbullah (Kramer 1993: 541–2). Suspicions about Iranian intrigue were exacerbated by Khomeini's statement: 'We will export our revolution to the four corners of the world because our revolution is Islamic, and the struggle will continue until the cry of *There is no god but God and Muhammad is His messenger* prevails throughout the world' (cited in Bernard & Khalilzad 1984: 148). President Rafsanjani was more explicit when he recommended to the Palestinians the tactic of hijacking an aircraft as a bargaining tool to free Palestinian prisoners in Israeli jails (*Middle East Journal* 1989: 22). Yet he tempered such declarations by statements such as, 'When we say we want to export our revolution, we do not want to do it with swords' (*Ibid*). Iranian activities were not limited to the Islamic world, for in January 1989 Khomeini sent an open letter to Gorbachov, in which the Soviet President was urged to abandon materialism and engage in serious study of Islam. (There is a parallel here with Muhammad sending letters to the rulers neighbouring Arabia). With regard to the activities in Lebanon, the Gulf States and the Palestinians, one has to have a certain degree of sympathy with the claim that the Iranian activities were in defence of deprived and severely neglected Muslims. Whether or not one agrees with the tactics that were adopted or advocated is another question.

The third issue concerns Khomeini's *fatwa* that authorized the execution of Salman Rushdie for his disrespect to Islam and Muhammad. From one perspective, the *fatwa* was issued to defend Islam, because for many Muslims, Rushdie's *Satanic Verses* was just another example of western arrogance, hostility towards Islam and prejudiced opinions that subsequently became increasingly anti-Islamic, especially after the Gulf War (Ahmad 1992: 185–91). (Khomeini's declaration of the *fatwa* against Rushdie has certain parallels with the example of Muhammad who ordered the execution of a female poet named Asma bint Marwan who composed verses which criticized him). This is not an attempt to exonerate Khomeini's *fatwa* (indeed, many leading Muslim scholars did not support it). However, it is necessary to understand *why* Khomeini felt it necessary to become involved in a controversy, which many in Britain would have preferred swept silently under the carpet. Rushdie was seen as a quisling, a Muslim who had been lured by the corruption of the West. For Muslims in the West, enough was enough: they were tired of racist attacks in London, and hearing derogatory statements from Le Pen, the French advocate of repatriation for French Muslims to North Africa. They considered Rushdie's 'apostasy' and 'insult' against Islam to be the final straw, and their demonstrations resounded in Iran and Pakistan where the issue was elevated to the international stage.

The question that assumes an almost *koanic* sense is where defensive *jihad* ends and offensive *jihad* starts. The meta-power enjoyed by the modern western world that sets most political, economic and social agendas is at the root of the problem. Most rhetoric that emerges from countries such as revolutionary Iran is not directed so much at establishing a world Islamic order, but rather it is a response to historical circumstance, economic weakness, and to the inequalities which separate the northern and southern spheres.

4 MODERN VIEWS OF *JIHAD* IN THE SUNNI WORLD

The nineteenth and twentieth centuries have posed great challenges to the Islamic world. Not only has the rational and largely secular world view of the western world seeped into most Muslim countries, but the majority of them have suffered from some form of occupation by the powers of Europe or by the United States. Although it appears that the Islamic response has become more vociferous in recent years, with calls for *jihad* whizzing daily through the channels of the media, M. Gilsenan rightly comments that 'there have been two hundred years of what Westerners treat as a ten-year wonder' (Gilsenan 1993: 18). The difference is that in the nineteenth century, the western colonial powers enjoyed a much freer hand in controlling areas where Islam prevailed, whereas after the second world war and the end of direct political manipulation, the 'nations-states' in the Islamic world could express their own desires. After 1945, western manipulation in these areas continued through economic and cultural channels, but in several of these nations, the secular and nationalist regimes that were based upon western models were rejected. From 1967 onwards it was realized that oil could be a weapon, Islam could be basis for government, and that the Islamic nations themselves would have to solve the Palestinian issue. Thus a new era of confidence in Islam emerged.

During this period of two hundred years, there have been many different interpretations of *jihad* and this section is an attempt to show the diversity of such interpretations. (A modern Shi'-ite interpretation of *jihad* was included in the previous section, so the following will focus upon several Sunni thinkers). There seems to be a consensus that the offensive (or military *jihad*) is no longer applicable, although the defensive *jihad* remains a duty for all Muslims. However, this does not mean that the goal of establishing Islam throughout the world has been abandoned. Just as Christians desire everyone to accept Jesus (in one form or another) and thus attain salvation, Muslims aspire to create an Islamic world order, established on the basis on reason and consent, by the pen and not the sword. This is the view of the Secretary-General of Hizbullah, Sayyid Hasan Nasrallah, who in 1994 admitted that he desired to see an Islamic state in Lebanon and beyond, but only if it could be established by dialogue and in an open atmosphere (Zisser 1997: 103–4).

Certain aspects relating to *jihad* and the concept of who should rule have already been mentioned in chapter one describing the ideas of Sayyid Ahmad Khan and Sayyid Abu Ala Mawdudi. In order to avoid repetition, the following section will present some of the ideas that have come out of Egypt in the modern period. First, the views of the 'Accommodationists'[5] will be described, and this will be followed by the interpretations of the 'Fundamentalists'.

At the beginning of the twentieth century, Egypt was nominally part of the Ottoman Empire. However, the British presence was prevalent in many governmental departments. Despite this, the most respected and learned Egyptian Muslim intellectuals of the late nineteenth century and early twentieth century interpreted *jihad* in quite a 'liberal' manner, typified in the works of Rashid Rida (1865–1935). Rida was the celebrated author of *al-Manar*, a journal that reflected the thought of Muhammad Abduh (who, as *mufti* of Egypt in 1899–1905, was the supreme official interpreter of Islamic law). There is no real difference between Rida's thought on *jihad* and that of Ahmad Khan. *Jihad* to spread Islam, according to Rida, is permissible only when the preaching of Islam is forbidden or Muslims are not allowed to live according to their law. Defensive *jihad,* however, is necessary at all times (Hourani 1983: 237).

A similar interpretation of *jihad*, written in 1933, was presented by Mahmud Shaltut who was the Rector of *al-Azhar* university in Cairo between 1958–63, the most prestigious religious-academic institution in the Sunni world. Shaltut offered a perspective of Islam that many nations, including the democratic and secular are happy to live with side by side. This is because his understanding of Islam is 'founded on the recognition of national states in the Islamic world, belonging to an international order based on peaceful relations' (R. Peters 1996: 59). Shaltut was aware of the changing global situation, including the centralization of the state and, therefore, the need to protect individual human rights. Moreover, increasing levels of contact between nations necessitated the regulation of international relations. Shaltut believed that guidelines to deal with such issues could be found in the Qur'an, which was revealed 'thirteen centuries before the human mind invented what is called the 'League of Nations' or the 'Security Council' to serve as a means of preservation of peace, consolidation of liberties and enjoyment by all states of their rights' (cited in R. Peters 1996: 72). Within his work entitled the *Muhammadan Mission and Fighting in Islam*, there are two central arguments that for Shaltut reveal the non-belligerent and non-coercive dimension of *jihad.*

First, Shaltut describes Islam as a religion that conforms to reason, and he cites several Qur'anic verses (11:28; 19:43–7; 20:43) in which the prophets Noah, Abraham, Moses, and Aaron speak of propagating the true religion through gentle persuasion and reason. He claims that Islam is the religion that conforms most of all to reason since it does not resort to miracles to prove its veracity, whereas other religions are accompanied by miracles of healing. This attempt to present Islam as a religion of logic and tolerance is supported with references from the Qur'an which state that any faith aroused by coercion is worthless in God's eyes, for *sura* 2:256 states: 'No compulsion is there in religion.'

The second significant discussion concerns those verses in the Qur'an which permit fighting and slaying. Shaltut claims that verses such as 22:39–41 (cited earlier) command Muslims to defend themselves, giving permission to those Muslims who were exiled from their homes by the Meccans and had thus lost their livelihood, and had to rebuild their lives from scratch in Medina.

One reason that explains the similarity in the interpretations of *jihad* given by Ahmad Khan, Abduh, Rida and Shaltut is that they were to greater and lesser extents limited and conditioned by high office and links with the state establishment which was tied to Britain. The Islamic world views of Ahmad Khan and

Abduh were also élitist and intellectual (verging on *Mu'tazilism*) and they were not concerned with creating a religious-political movement for the masses. Of course these thinkers desired to educate Muslims, but their reforms affected only a small percentage of the population.

The views of the Islamic revivalists or fundamentalists are different to those offered by Shaltut. One of the earliest examples of the fundamentalist position is provided in a short treatise entitled *Jihad* by Hasan al-Banna, written during the 1940s. Hasan al-Banna was the founder of the Muslim Brotherhood, the largest of the so-called Islamic fundamentalists groups in Egypt. Therefore his contribution to the continuing analysis on *jihad* should be taken seriously. His views on *jihad*, and those of his followers are different from the more liberal interpretations perhaps due to their disassociation from high office, and their policies of creating units of Muslims at grass roots level.

Within his treatise, Banna states that the requirement to participate in *jihad* is expressed in the Qur'an, *hadith*, and also in the books of the Islamic jurists, and in this respect, his arguments do not differ from other contemporary Muslims. However, he despaired about the situation of Egypt. Although not declaring Egypt *dar al-harb*, he came very close to doing so:

> Today, my brother, the Muslims as you know are forced to be subservient before others and are ruled by disbelievers. Our lands have been besieged, and our dignity violated. Our enemies are overlooking our affairs, and the rites of our religion are under their jurisdiction. Yet still the Muslims fail to fulfil the responsibility of mission that is on their shoulders. Hence in this situation it becomes the duty of each and every Muslim to make *jihad*.
>
> (al-Banna 1996: 28)

On the basis of such arguments, it is possible to interpret Banna's ideas as concentrating upon the defensive *jihad*. However, his citation and interpretation of certain Qur'anic verses suggest he views world-Islam as the goal, although this is to be implemented peacefully through teaching:

> Islam allows *jihad* and permits war until the following Qur'anic verse is fulfilled:
>
> > We will show them Our signs in the horizons, and in their selves, until it becomes manifest to them that this [the Qur'an] is the truth. (41:53)
>
> People have for some time now ridiculed this but today these same people acknowledge that preparation for war is the surest way to peace! Allah did not ordain *jihad* for the Muslims so that it may be used as a tool for oppression or tyranny or so that it may be used by some to further their personal gains. Rather *jihad* is used to safeguard the mission of spreading Islam. This would guarantee peace and the means of implementing the Supreme Message.
>
> (Ibid.: 29)

However, the idea of spreading Islam throughout the world was not a realistic goal, but Hasan al-Banna and the Muslim Brotherhood were concerned about defending the whole of the *dar al-islam*, not just Egypt, from non-Muslim influence. This became particularly acute in the late 1930s when Lord Peel recommended the partition of Palestine. In support of the Palestinians, their fellow Muslims and Arabs, the Muslim Brotherhood raised funds and published articles in the press denouncing the British (Lia 1998: 235–47).

One interesting development in the policy of the Muslim Brotherhood concerned whether or not the *jihad* could be carried out against the Egyptian government itself. Although Hasan al-Banna never endorsed a *jihad* against the Egyptian state, the Muslim Brotherhood, as represented by Sayyid Qutb (d. 1966) certainly indicated that this was the case. Qutb viewed Egyptian society as a *jahiliyya* society, that is, a society steeped in ignorance, comparable to that of Arabia prior to Muhammad:

> Any society that is not Muslim is *jahiliyya*...as is any society in which something other than God alone is worshipped...Thus, we must include in this category all the societies that now exist on earth.
>
> (Cited in Kepel 1984: 47)

The logical conclusion to such an argument was to fight against *jahiliyya*, just as Muhammad had fought against the unbelievers, and this was the interpretation that was taken up by the Islamic groups that mushroomed in Egypt from the 1960s onwards. One such group, led by Shukri Mustafa who claimed that Egyptian society was *jahiliyya* and therefore its citizens were unbelievers (ibid.: 74), was called the Society of Muslims. Ultimately, some of the members of this group kidnapped and executed a former minister of religious affairs. Shukri's non-recognition of the Egyptian state resulted in his claim that he would not join a defensive *jihad*, that is, even if the Egyptian forces were attacked by the Jews (ibid.: 84).

The event that brought such 'fundamentalist' groups to the attention of the western public was the assassination of President Sadat in 1981. The group that carried out this act was named *al-Jihad*, and like the Society of Muslims, its members believed that the rulers in Egypt were apostates from Islam. The 'ideologue' of the group, Abd al-Salam Faraj was also inspired by the writings of Sayyid Qutb, and his own works cited passages from Qutb in which he encouraged people to fulfil their duty of *jihad* on behalf of God (Jansen 1986: 30, 226). In a document published by *al-Jihad*, it is noted that some individuals believe that *jihad* against Israel should be the priority. However this is rejected for three reasons. First, *jihad* against the enemy at home takes precedence over everything. Second, *jihad* must be waged by an Islamic ruler, in other words, it is illegal to participate in a *jihad* which is being lead by an infidel Egyptian government. Third, the existence of colonialism or imperialism lies with the present Egyptian state, therefore to wage *jihad* against the imperialists must begin with the infidel at home (Jansen 1997: 124). This is the logic behind recent terrorist attacks in Egypt such as the bombing at the Egyptian museum in Cairo and at Luxor in the summer and autumn of 1997. These events were aimed at undermining the Egyptian state; by threatening the tourist trade, the Egyptian economy would weaken, and foundations of the Egyptian state would be shaken.

CONCLUSION

Peaceful coexistence between Islamic and non-Islamic states does not have to be threatened by the concept of *jihad*. The west's ignorance about *jihad* (and Islam in general) is, of course, the greatest barrier to initiate peaceful co-existence. It is surprising to find levels of ignorance even among those individuals who should know better. The masculine side of Islam (emphasizing God's wrath, anger, majesty, and the Lesser *jihad*) is all too often stressed over and above the feminine dimension, which portrays God's mercy, compassion, love and intimacy. The following is a typical example:

> Some of the most beautiful names in the human language are given to the God of the Koran, but He is ultimately a God outside of the world, a God who is *only Majesty, never Emmanuel*, God-with-us.

This distorted view of Islam, expressed by Pope John Paul II (1994: 92), reveals that he is unacquainted with *sura* 57:4: 'He is with you wherever you are,' and *sura* 50:16: 'We are nearer to Him than the jugular vein.' Harmony is established by balancing masculine and feminine dimensions of *jihad*. Such a view is contained in the comments of A. Ahmad, a contemporary Islamic scholar based in Britain: '*Jihad* has become a dirty word in the media, representing the physical threat of a barbaric civilization. Yet the concept is noble and powerful. It is the desire to improve oneself, to attempt betterment and to struggle for the good cause. It is Tennysonian in its scope: to strive, to seek and not to yield' (Ahmad 1992: 42).[6]

The concept of *jihad*, and Islam itself is not a monolithic entity threatening the western world, and the diversity within Islam was revealed during the Gulf War. Thankfully there have been several studies that have exposed the myth of Islamic confrontation with the west. For example, B. Lawrence writes: 'Lame and ludicrous is the effort of polemicists like Frances Fukuyama and Samuel Huntington to portray Muslim governments as both unified and adamant in opposing the West and Western interests' (Lawrence 1998: 162).

All too often, the opinions of liberal Islamic intellectuals, such as Fazlur Rahman, Abdul Karim Soroush, and Mahmoud Mohamad Taha are overshadowed by 'fundamentalists'. Such individuals are keen to preserve their Islamic culture and heritage which means that on occassions Islam needs to be protected from the excesses of Western culture. However, they are also quick to point out that Islam is not inherently hostile to rationality, Christianity, or the West. Indeed, Mahmoud Mohamad Taha (a Sudanese intellectual who was executed in the 1980s) argued that *jihad* 'is not an original precept in Islam' (Kurzman 1998: 274). Furthermore, one of Fazlur Rahman's main arguments is that it is necessary to engage in a systematic analysis of the verses of the Qur'an in the order in which they were revealed, and study them in historical context. In other words, the specific commandments of the Qur'an should be understood in the light of the universal meaning of the Qur'an, which includes respect for other religions and peaceful co-existence. Rahman also offers a definition of *jihad* 'intellectual *jihad*', otherwise known as *ijtihad*, which denotes *jihad* 'the effort to understand the meaning of a relevant text or precedent in the past, containing a rule, and to alter that rule by extending or restricting or otherwise modifying it in such a manner that a new situation can be subsumed under it by a new solution' (Rahman 1984: 7–8).

Many of the modern Muslim interpretations of *jihad* outlined in this chapter endorse the system of nation-states based upon international law. Such interpretations, one presumes, also reformulate issues related to *dhimmis* to accord with equal rights. (In fact *dhimmi* status was abrogated within the Ottoman Empire and Egypt in the nineteenth century—the *jizyah* was abolished in 1855–6). Some modern Egyptian writers have argued for a new jurisprudence that does not bifurcate society between Muslims and Christians (Haddad 1995: 381–98). However the fear and suspicion felt by Egyptian Copts increased due to the establishment of Islamic law as the main source of Egyptian legislation in 1980.

Even those Islamic thinkers who are not prepared to give equal rights to *dhimmis,* such as Mawdudi, envisage an Islamic world order created not by the sword but by the pen, preaching and persuasion. Such methods are unlikely to cause many sleepless nights for non-Islamic western politicians. More serious however, are the calls for *jihad* (including those that are implicit) that echo from revivalist movements in Egypt and Iran. Although these movements were and still are a response to the internal situations of those countries, the western powers were and still are responsible in shaping those circumstances to varying degrees. This is not to say that the emergence of Islamic revivalism is attributable exclusively to the policies of western powers. Other factors such as the reaction to modernity, the social dislocations concomitant with rapid urbanization, corruption within Islamic states, and an unhealthy and excessive attachment to tradition must also be considered. However, the call for *jihad*, either against the *jahiliyya* states, or against the unbelievers, should warn the non-Islamic western world to reflect on its own policies in the international world.
Increasing levels of immigration and the emergence of a global culture means that the existence of Islam is a reality that the west will have to deal with more and more. This being the case, it is advisable for Muslims, Christians, and those of a purely secular persuasion to reflect on Rumi's words:

If you see an ugly face, 'tis you! And if you see Jesus and Mary, 'tis you!

(Rumi 1925–40: I, 245)

NOTES

1. *See*, J. Hooper's article in *The Guardian*, 22 April 1998, p. 11.
2. *Ibid.*
3. Doubt has been cast on the authenticity of this tradition, *see,* Watt 1961: 194. For the text of these letters *see*, Khadduri 1979: 241–42.

4. Aqa Sayyid Muhammad Isfahani agitated for *jihad* from the Ottoman city of Karbala, while in Sultaniyya, the clergy issued a *fatwa* declaring opposition to *jihad* was unbelief. *See*, F. Kazemzadeh 1991: 714.
5. Muhammad Abduh and Rashid Rida have also been called 'founding fathers of Islamic fundamentalism,' *see*, Jansen 1997: 40.
6. The 'Tennysonian' reference is to the end of Tennyson's poem *Ulysses*:
   Tho' much is taken, much abides; and tho'
   We are not now that strength which in old days
   Moved earth and heaven, that which we are, we are,
   One equal temper of heroic hearts
   Made weak by time and fate, but strong in will
   To strive, to seek, to find, and not to yield.

Bibliography

Adams, C. (1983) 'Mawdudi and the Islamic State,' in J. Esposito (ed.), *Voices of Resurgent Islam*, Oxford: Oxford University Press.

Agwani, M. (1996) 'God's Government: Jama'at-i-Islami in India,' in H. Mutalib (ed.), *Islam, Muslims and the Modern State,* London: MacMillan.

Ahmad, A. (1960-1) 'Sayyid Ahmad Khan, Jamal al-Din al-Afghani and Muslim India,' *Studia Islamica*, XIII-XIV.

_____, (1967) *Islamic Modernism in India and Pakistan 1857-1964*, Oxford: Oxford Univesity Press.

Ahmad, A. S. (1992) *Postmodernism and Islam,* London: Routledge.

Ahmad, M. (1991) 'Islamic Fundamentalism in South Asia,' in Marty & Appleby (ed.), *Fundamentalism Observed*, Chicago: Chicago University Press.

Akter Banu, R. (1996) 'Jamaat-i-Islami in Bangladesh: Challenges and Politics,' in H. Mutalib, *Islam, Muslims and the Modern State*, London: Macmillan.

Al-Azmeh, A. (1993) *Islams and Modernities*, London: Verso.

Ali, A. (1891) *The Spirit of Islam*, London: W. H. Allen & Co.

Arberry, A. (1991a) *Mystical Poems of Rumi 1*, Chicago: University of Chicago Press.

_____, (1991b) *Mystical Poems of Rumi* 2, Chicago: University of Chicago Press.

Austin, R. (1980) *Ibn al-Arabi: The Bezels of Wisdom*, New York: Paulist Press.

Awn, P. (1983) *Satan's Tragedy and Redemption: Iblis in Sufi Psychology*, Leiden: Brill.

'Ayn al-Qudat (1373) *Tamhidat,* A. Osseiran (ed.), Tehran: Intisharat-I Manuchihri.

Ayoub, M. (1992) 'Jihad: A Source of Power and Framework of Authority in Islam,' in *Bulletin of the Institute of Middle Eastern Studies,* International University of Japan, Niigata, vol. VI.

Baljon, J. (1949) *The Reforms and Religious Ideas of Sir Sayyid Ahmad Khan*, Leiden: Brill.

al-Banna, H. (1996) *Jihad,* London: International Islamic Forum.

Bernard, C. & Khalilzad, Z. (1984) *The Government of God*, New York: Columbia University Press.

Bowering, G. (1980) *The Mystical Vision of Existence in Classical Islam*, New York: Walter de Gruyter.

Cahen, C. (1968) (trans. J. Jones-Williams), *Pre-Ottoman Turkey,* London: Sidgwick & Jackson.

Chittick, W. (1983) *The Sufi Path of Love,* Albany: SUNY Press.

Christie-Murray, D. (1989) *A History of Heresy*, Oxford: Oxford University Press.

Corbin, H. (1994) *The Man of Light in Iranian Sufism*, (trans. N. Pearson), New York: Omega Publications.

——, (1969) *Creative Imagination in the Sufism of Ibn 'Arabi*, (trans. R. Manheim), New Jersey: Princeton University Press.

Dabashi, H. (1994) 'Rumi and the Problems of Theodicy: Moral Imagination and Narrative Discourse in a Story of the *Masnavi*,' in Banani, Houannisian & Sabagh (eds.), *Poetry and Mysticism in Islam*, Cambridge: Cambridge University Press.

Dostoyevski, F. (1985) *The House of the Dead* (trans. D. McDuff), London: Penguin Books.

Edwards, D. (1986) 'Shi'i Political Dissent in Afghanistan', in J. Cole & N. Keddie (eds), *Shi'ism and Social Protest*, New Haven: Yale University Press.

Epstein, I. (1987) *Sanhedrin,* London: The Soncino Press.

Enayat, H. (1982) *Modern Islamic Political Thought*, Austin: University of Texas Press.

Ernst, C. (1997) *The Shambhala Guide to Sufism*, Boston & London: Shambhala.

——, (1985) *Words of Ecstasy in Sufism,* Albany: SUNY Press.

Fakhri, M. (1983) *A History of Islamic Philosophy,* London: Longman.

Fisk, R. (1998) 'US Media Mirror Distorts Middle East,' in *The Independent*, 10.06.98.

Friedmann, Y. (1989) *Prophecy Continuous: Aspects of Ahmadi Religious Thought and Its Medieval Background,* Berkeley: University of California Press.

Furuzanfar, B. (1982) *Ahadith mathnawi*, Tehran: Amir Kabir.

Gandhi, R. (1986) *Understanding the Muslim Mind*, New Delhi: Penguin.

Gibb, H. A. R. (1947) *Modern Trends in Islam*, Chicago: University of Chicago Press.

Gilsenan, M. (1993) *Recognising Islam*, London: I. B. Tauris.

Goodman, L. (1972) *Ibn Tufayl's Hayy Ibn Yaqzan*, New York: Twayne Publishers.

Graham, W. (1977) *Divine Word and Prophetic Word in Early Islam*, The Hague: Mouton.

Haddad, Y. (1995) 'Christians in a Muslim State,' in *Christian-Muslim Encounters,* Gainesville: University Press of Florida.

Halliday, F. (1996) *Islam and the Myth of Confrontation*, London: I. B. Tauris.

Hastie, W. (1903) *The Festival of Spring from the Divan of Jalal ed-Din*, Glasgow: J. MacLehose & Sons.

Hick, J. (1996) *Evil and the God of Love,* London: Macmillan.

Hiro, D. (1988) *Islamic Fundamentalism*, London: Paladin.

Hooper, J. (1998) *The Guardian*, April 14.

Hourani, A. (1962) *Arabic Thought in the Liberal Age,* Cambridge: Cambridge University Press.

Hujwiri (1375) *Kashf al-Mahjub*, Zhukovski (ed), Tehran: Kitabkhana-yi turi.

______, (1976) *Kashf al-Mahjub of al-Hujwiri*, (trans. R. Nicholson), London: Luzac & Co.

Ibn Ishaq (1955) *The Life of Muhammad* (trans. A. Guillaume), Oxford: Oxford University Press.

Ibn Kathir (1981) *Mukhtasar Tafsir Ibn Kathir*, Muhammad 'Ali al-Sabuni (ed.), Beirut: Dar al-Qur'an al-Karim.

Irenaeus (1997) *Against Heresies* (trans. R. Grant), in *Irenaeus of Lyons*, London: Routledge.

Jameelah, M. (1962) *Islam Versus the West*, Delhi: Sh. Muhammad Ashraf.

Jansen, J. J. G. (1986) *The Neglected Duty*, New York: Macmillan.

______, (1997) *The Dual Nature of Islamic Fundamentalism,* London: Hurst.

Jeffrey, A. (1929) 'Muhammad: Real and Unreal,' *International Review of Missions*, Vol XVIII.

John-Paul II (1994) *Crossing the Threshold of Hope,* London: Jonathan Cape.

Johnson, J. T. (1977) *The Holy War in Western and Islamic Tradition*, Pennsylvania: Penn State Press.

Kazemzadeh, F. (1991) 'Iranian Relations with Russia and the Soviet Union to 1921,' in *The Cambridge History of Iran*, vol. VII. Cambridge: Cambridge University Press.

Kepel, G. (1985) *The Prophet and Pharaoh* (trans. J. Rothschild), London: Al-Saqi Books.

Khadduri, M. (1979) *War and Peace in the Law of Islam*, New York: AMS Press.

Khan, A. (1993) *Political Profile of Sir Sayyid Ahmad Khan,* H. Malik (ed.), Delhi: Adam Publishers.

Khomeini, R. (1985) *Islam and Revolution* (translated and annotated by H. Algar), London: KPI.

King, J. R. (1990) 'Jesus and Joseph in Rumi's Mathnawi,' *The Muslim World*, 80/2.

Kiyani, M. (1990) *Tarikh-i khanaqah dar iran,* Tehran: Kitabkhana-yi Tahuri.

Kohlberg, E. (1976) 'The Development of the Imami Shi'i Doctrine of Jihad,' *Zeitschrift Der Deutschen Morgenlandischen Gesellschaft.*

Kramer, M. (1993) 'Hizbullah: The Calculus of Jihad,' in Marty and Appleby (eds.), *Fundamentalisms and the State,* Chicago: University of Chicago Press.

Kubra, N. (1361) *Al-Sa'ir al-ha'ir,* M. Qasimi (ed), Tehran: Kitabfurushi Zawwar.

Kurzman, C. (ed.) (1998) *Liberal Islam*, Oxford: Oxford University Press.

Lambton, A. (1981) *State and Government in Medieval Islam*, Oxford: Oxford University Press.

Lawrence, B. (1998) *Shattering the Myth: Islam Beyond Violence,* New Jersey: Princeton University Press.

Lazarus-Yafeh, H. (1992) *Intertwined Worlds*, New Jersey: Princeton University Press.

Lia, B. (1998) *The Society of Muslim Brothers in Egypt,* Reading: Ithaca Press.

Mahmoud, M. (1997) 'Sufism and Islamism in the Sudan,' in Westerlund & Rosander (eds.), *African Islam and Islam in Africa,* London: Hurst.

Majeed, J. (1998) 'Nature, Hyperbole and the Colonial State,' in J. Cooper, R. Nettler & M Mahmoud (eds.), *Islam and Modernity,* London: I. B. Tauris.

Malik, S. (1972) 'Religious and Economic Factors in 19th Century India,' *Islamic Culture*, 46/1.

Mason, H. (1995) *Hallaj*, Richmond: Curzon Press.

Massignon, L. (1994) *Hallaj: Mystic and Martyr* (translated, edited and abridged by H. Mason), New Jersey: Princeton University Press.

Mawdudi, M. (1982) *Let Us Be Muslims,* Leicester: Islamic Foundation.

______, (1988-9) *Towards Understanding the Qur'an* (trans. Zafar Ishaq Ansari), Leicester: The Islamic Foundation.

McAuliffe, J. (1991) *Qur'anic Christians*, Cambridge: Cambridge University Press.

McDonough,. S. (1984) *Muslim Ethics and Modernity*, Ontario: Wilfrid Laurier University Press.

Meier, F. (1960) 'The Spiritual Man in the Persian Poet 'Attar', in J. Campbell (ed.), *Spiritual Disciplines: Papers from the Eranos Yearbook*, New Jersey: Princeton University Press.

______, (1954) 'The nature of monism in Islam', in J. Campbell (ed.) *Eranos Yearbook*, New York.

Mesle, C. (1991) *John Hick's Theodicy,* London: Macmillan.

Metcalf, B. (1982) *Islamic Revival in British India*, New Jersey: Princeton University Press.

Minns, D. (1994) *Irenaeus,* London: Geoffrey Chapman.

Moorhouse, G. (1983) *India Britannica*, London: W. Collins & Co. Ltd.

Mubarak, A. (1978) *Kitab al-Jihad*, ed. Nazih Hammad, Tunis: al-Dar al-Tunisiyah lil-Nashr.

Najm al-Din Razi (1982) *The Path of God's Bondsmen From Origin to Return* (trans. H Algar), New York: Caravan Books.

Nasafi, A. (1963) *al-Insan al-Kamil*, M. Molé (ed.), Tehran/ Paris: Maisonneuve.

——, (1965) *Kashf al-haqa'iq*, M. Damghani (ed.), Tehran: Bungah-i tarjuma wa nashr-i kitab.

——, (1973) *Maqsad-i aqsa,* appended to Jami's *Ashi''at al-lama'at*, H Rabbani (ed.), Tehran: Kitabkhana-yi 'ilmiyya-yi hamidi.

——, (1985) *Zubdat al-haqa'iq*, Haqq-wardi Nasiri (ed.), Tehran: Kitabkhana-yi tahuri.

—— *Kitab-i tanzil*, Manchester University, John Rylands Library, C112, fol. 75a, lines 1-5.

Nasr, S. H. (1994) *A Young Muslim's Guide to the Modern World*, Chicago: Kazi Publications.

——, (1996) *The Islamic Intellectual Tradition in Persia,* Richmond: Curzon Press.

Nasr, S. R. V. (1994) *The Vanguard of the Islamic Revolution: The Jama'at-i Islami of Pakistan*, London: I. B. Tauris.

——, (1996) *Mawdudi and the Making of Islamic Revolution*, Oxford: Oxford University Press.

Nicholson, R. A. (1898) *Selected Poems from the Divani Shamsi Tabriz,* Cambridge: Cambridge University Press.

——, (1925-40) *Mathnawi of Jalalu'ddin Rumi: Vol. I & II Commentary*, London, Luzac.

——, (1950) *Rumi, Mystic and Poet*, London: George Allen and Unwin.

Ormsby, E. (1984) *Theodicy in Islamic Thought*, New Jersey: Princeton University Press.

Parrinder, G. (1995) *Jesus in the Qur'an*, Oxford: One World.

Partner, P. (1997) *God of Battles,* London: HarperCollins.

Peters, F. E. (1990) *Judaism, Christianity and Islam: The Classical Texts and Their Interpretation*, Vol. I. New Jersey: Princeton University Press, 1990.

Peters, R. (1996) *Jihad in Classical and Modern Islam*, Princeton: Markus Wiener Publishers.

Pfander, K. (1986) *The Mizan-al-haqq: Balance of Truth,* Villach, Austria

Powell, A. (1976) 'Maulana Rahmat Allah Kairanawi and Muslim Christian Controversy in India in the mid 19th Century,' *Journal of the Royal Asiatic Society.*

Rahman, F. (1984) *Islam and Modernity*, Chicago: University of Chicago Press.

Ramazani, R. (1988) *Revolutionary Iran*, London: Johns Hopkins.

Ranstorp, M. (1997) *Hizb'allah in Lebanon*, London: Macmillan.

Razavi, M. (1997) *Suhrawardi and the School of Illumination*, Richmond: Curzon.

Renard, J. (1994) *All the King's Falcons,* Albany: SUNY Press.

Ridgeon, L. (1998a) *'Aziz Nasafi*, Richmond: Curzon Press.

______, (1998b) 'A Sufi Perspective of Evil,' *Iran* (Journal of the British Institute of Persian Studies), vol. XXXVI.

Rumi (1925–40) *Mathnawi-yi ma'nawi*, 6 vols, R. A. Nicholson (ed.), Leiden: Brill.

______, (1957–66) *Kulliyat-i Shams* (or *Diwan-i Shams)*, B. Furuzanfar (ed.), ten volumes, Tehran: University of Tehran Press.

______, (1993) *Fihi ma fihi*, (trans. A. J. Arberry as *Discourses of Rumi*), Richmond: Curzon Press.

Sachedina, A. (1988) *The Just Ruler in Shi'ite Islam*, Oxford: Oxford University Press.

Sambursky, S. (1987) *The Physical World of the Greeks*, London: Routledge.

Schimmel, A. (1980) *The Triumphal Sun*, London & The Hague: East-West Publications.

______, (1994a) *Deciphering the Signs of God*, Albany: SUNY Press.

______, (1994b) *Foreward* in J Renard, *All the King's Falcons.*

Schleifer, S. (1984) 'Jihad: Sacred Struggle in Islam,' *Islamic Quarterly.*

Schwarz, M. (1972) 'Acquistion *(Kasb)* in Early Islam,' in *Islamic Philosophy and the Classical Tradition,* Oxford: Cassirer.

Scott-Clark, C. & Levy, A. (1999) 'Beyond Belief,' in *The Sunday Times Magazine*, 24.1.99, London.

Smith, W. (1946) *Modern Islam in India*, London: Victor Gollancz Ltd.

Suhrawardi (1973) 'Risalat al-futuwwa,' in *Risa'il-i Jawanmardan*, M. Sarraf (ed.), Tehran/Paris: Maisonneuve.

Sulami (1953) *Kitab Tabaqat al-sufiyya*, Nur al-Din Shurayba (ed.), Cairo: Jama'at al-azhar li'l-nashr wa al-ta'lif.

Symonds, R. (1987) *The Making of Pakistan*, Lahore: Islamic Book Service.

Thomas, D. (2000) 'The Doctrine of the Trinity in the Early Abbasid Era', in *Islamic Interpretations of Christianity*, L. Ridgeon (ed.), Richmond: Curzon Press.

Troll, C. (1978a) *Sayyid Ahmad Khan: A Reinterpretation of Muslim Theology,* New Delhi: Vikas.

______, (1978b) 'Sir Sayyid Ahmad Khan, 1817-98, and his Theological Critics,' *Islamic Culture*, 52/2.

______, (1985) 'A Note on the Tafsir-i Thana'i of Thana Allah Amritsari and his Criticism of Sayyid Ahmad Khan's Tafsir-i-Ahmadi,' *Islamic Culture*, 59.

Van der Mehden, F. (1983) 'American Perceptions of Islam,' in J. Esposito (ed), *Voices of Resurgent Islam*, Oxford: Oxford University Press.

Waley, M. (1991) 'Najm al-Din Kubra and the Central Asian School of Sufism (The Kubrawiyyah)' in S. H. Nasr (ed.), *Islamic Spirituality: Manifestations*, London: SCM Press.

Watt, W. (1948) *Free will and Pre destination in Early Islam,* London: Luzac & Co.

______, (1961) *Muhammad: Prophet and Statesman,* Oxford: Oxford University Press.

_____, (1962) *Islamic Philosophy and Theology,* Edinburgh: Edinburgh University Press.

_____, (1976) 'Islamic Conceptions of the Holy War,' in Thomas Patrick Murphy (ed), *The Holy War,* Columbus: Ohio State University Press.

_____, (1991) *Muslim-Christian Encounters*, London: Routledge.

Zisser, E. (1997) 'Hizballah in Lebanon,' in Maddy-Weitzman & Inbar (eds), *Religious Radicalism in the Greater Middle East*, London: Frank Cass.

Zobairi, R. (1983) 'Sir Syed Ahmad Khan's Interpretation of Muslim Society and His Reform Movement in the Indian Context,' *Islamic Culture*, 57.